THEOLOGY AND THE LGBTQ+ COMMUNITY

THEOLOGY AND THE LGBTQ+ COMMUNITY

HISTORICAL PERSPECTIVES AND CONTEMPORARY CHALLENGES

LUÍS CORRÊA LIMA, SJ

TRANSLATED BY SUZANA REGINA MOREIRA

Paulist Press
New York / Mahwah, NJ

Cover image by kropekk_pl/Pixabay.com
Cover design by Joe Gallagher
Book design by Lynn Else

Originally published in Portuguese as *Teologia e os LGBT+, perspectiva histórica e desafios contemporâneos* by Editora Vozes in Brazil, copyright © 2021.

Editorial observation: some direct quotations have been freely translated for this English edition.

Library of Congress Cataloging-in-Publication Data
Names: Lima, Luís Corrêa, author. | Moreira, Suzana Regina, translator.
Title: Theology and the LGBTQ+ community: historical perspectives and contemporary challenges / Luís Corrêa Lima, SJ; translated by Suzana Regina Moreira.
Other titles: Teologia e os LGBT+. English
Description: New York, Mahwah, NJ: Paulist Press, [2025] | Translation of: Teologia e os LGBT+ : perspectiva histórica e desafios contemporâneos. | Includes bibliographical references and index. | Summary: "This book is a rereading of the Judeo-Christian tradition and the teaching of the Catholic Church aimed at the inclusion and citizenship of the LGBTQ+ population"—Provided by publisher.
Identifiers: LCCN 2024010230 (print) | LCCN 2024010231 (ebook) | ISBN 9780809157075 (paperback) | ISBN 9780809188710 (e-book)
Subjects: LCSH: Church work with gay people–Catholic Church. | Church and minorities. | Sexual minorities—Religious life. | Catholic Church—Doctrines.
Classification: LCC BX1795.H66 L5613 2025 (print) | LCC BX1795.H66 (ebook) | DDC 259.086/64—dc23/eng/20240906
LC record available at https://lccn.loc.gov/2024010230
LC ebook record available at https://lccn.loc.gov/2024010231

ISBN 978-0-8091-5707-5 (paperback)
ISBN 978-0-8091-8871-0 (e-book)

Published by Paulist Press
997 Macarthur Boulevard
Mahwah, New Jersey 07430
www.paulistpress.com

Printed and bound in the
United States of America

To Sister Jeannine Gramick, SL, my main inspiration

CONTENTS

FOREWORD

GENERAL CURIA OF THE SOCIETY OF JESUS

Esteemed Fr. Luís Corrêa Lima,

Thank you for being so kind to send me your recent book, *Teologia e os LGBT+, perspectiva histórica e desafios contemporâneos* (Editora Vozes, 2021). It is a work that undoubtedly gathers the fruits of your many years of pastoral accompaniment to LGBT+ people, as well as of your fruitful academic activity at the Pontifical Catholic University of Rio de Janeiro, especially in the research group "Sexual Diversity—Citizenship and Religion," of which you are the coordinator.

Your book has many merits. First, it succinctly presents—but without simplifications—the fundamental elements of Catholic Theology and the Magisterium on the subject in question, while continuing to make a critical and updated reading of these elements, thus opening the space for a serious and dispassionate reflection and for a mature and sincere dialogue on issues that deeply touch the lives of so many people in their experience of faith.

In this way, your work is certainly presented as an instrument that favors the understanding of the reality of LGBT+ people in their relationship with faith, with God, and with the Church. By providing a reflection on the existential reality of these people with spirituality, moral theology, biblical exegesis, and Christian anthropology, your book offers quality information as an opportunity for reflection for all those who wish to better understand this reality to live it in a better evangelical way.

Pope Paul VI, in his address to the Society at General Congregation 32, said: "Wherever in the Church, even in the most difficult and extreme fields, in the crossroads of ideologies, in the front line of social conflict, there has been and there is a confrontation between the deepest desires of man and the perennial message of the Gospel, there also have been, and there are, Jesuits." I believe that the apostolic service that you render to the Church and society by accompanying people who live the LGBT+ reality is an experience that confirms those words of the late Pope Paul VI.

I ask the Father, with His grace, to continue supporting your apostolic service in the following of His Son and that you always count on the lights of the Spirit in your commitment to bring people closer to the kingdom of God.

Fraternally in Christ Jesus,

Fr. Arturo Sosa, SJ
General Superior
Rome, September 3, 2021

INTRODUCTION

My involvement with the LGBTQ+ community and with this topic came out of my priestly ministry. Over many years I've met people born and raised in the Catholic Church who over time found themselves that way. They realized they had such deep-rooted characteristics that are constitutive of their being and part of their identity. This realization was not without pain and painful conflicts, including with one's own faith and ecclesiastical membership. Fortunately, I found open paths to carry out an apostolate with these people, as well as to deepen reflection on their reality. The Society of Jesus, the religious order to which I belong, supported me. At the Pontifical Catholic University of Rio de Janeiro (PUC-Rio), where I am a professor and researcher, the possibility arose of forming a research group, registered with the National Research Council (CNPq), on sexual and gender diversity, citizenship, and religion.

In this way, the apostolate continued along with the study and publication of many texts and articles on the subject. At a certain point, an invitation was extended to publish a book. I realized that it was an opportunity to elaborate something more comprehensive about theology and the LGBTQ+ community, in order to gather, articulate, and deepen ideas that until then were dispersed across different publications.

The work begins by considering sexuality and its relationship with the Judeo-Christian tradition. This is the fundamental starting point for thinking about theology in the face of the issues raised recently by gender studies, which include sexual orientation. This follows with a historical overview of the emergence of these issues, the configuration of LGBTQ+ citizenship, and the positions of the Catholic world in this regard. Non-Catholic Christianity also deserves consideration, but given the vastness of the topic, it was not possible to do so in this work. A chapter is devoted to the issue of access by homosexual people to the priestly ministry, given the current relevance of the subject. The final chapter focuses on theological perspectives and challenges, as well as possible pastoral paths.

Thinking about the reality of the LGBTQ+ population from a theological perspective requires, first, to be sensitized by their pains and conflicts, as well as to recognize their talents, contributions, and possibilities. All this comes to the fore with the visibility of this population. In many countries, there is a strong aversion to this population that produces various forms of physical, verbal, and symbolic violence. There are parents who say: "I prefer a dead son to a gay son." It is not uncommon for gays and lesbians to be expelled from home by their parents. Among the most offensive swear words that exist in Portuguese are references to the homosexual condition and anal intercourse, which is common in male homoeroticism—in other words, it's an insult. Often, when one says: "so-and-so is not a man," it is understood that he is gay; or "so-and-so is not a woman," it is understood that she is a lesbian. That is, being a man or being a woman supposedly excludes the homosexual person, relegated to sub-humanity. In Brazil, homicides are frequent, especially of transgender persons. There is also the suicide of many teenagers and even adults, who discover that they are gay or lesbian. They arrive at this extreme attitude because they sense the hostile rejection of their own family and society. Homophobia and transphobia run deep in the culture. Such hostility generates countless forms of discrimination and, even if it does not lead to death, it often brings deep sadness or depression.

In the Christian world, quotes from the Bible are often taken out of context or made with undue simplifications of doctrine and directed at the LGBTQ+ community with extreme rigidity and condemnation. Sometimes they are considered demon-possessed and in need of being exorcised or subjected to prayers of "healing and deliverance" to change their condition or identity. Consequently, the proclamation of the Gospel, which is good news, does not heal wounds or warm the heart but brings more devastation. The word of the God of life becomes the word of death.

This situation of oppression leads me to share a dramatic experience that I had a few years ago. I went to a same-sex law symposium at the Catholic University of Pernambuco. In front of a crowded and vibrant auditorium, I participated in a roundtable. I spoke about the love of God and the importance of one's conscience. And I warned about the misuse that is often made of the Bible to condemn homosexuals. Afterward, a young man came to me and said: "Father, you don't know the good you've done to me! I was going to kill myself! I even wrote a farewell letter to my family, which is here in my backpack." I was stunned. I chatted briefly with him, got his contact and gave him mine. I earnestly asked that from that day forward we keep in touch. I returned to Rio de Janeiro. Three days later, the young man wrote to me with his story:

> I was raised in the Church. My mother is a minister of the Eucharist. The place where I most like to be is the Church. Because I'm gay, my parish priest gave a tough sermon at a mass. Looking at me, he said that homosexual people have a demon. The longer they live, the more they sin. It is better that they do not live long. And the other worshipers nodded their heads in agreement. From listening to this so much, and from seeing others agree, I made a decision: "this demon here is not going to live anymore!" I decided that, on September 17, 2011, I would go to an eighteen-story public building and throw myself from the top. I wrote a letter to my family and put it in my backpack. When that day dawned, I took the bus to the place. However, I met a friend on the bus who told me: "We are going to the Catholic (University) symposium." I didn't want to go, but my friend insisted. I accepted because the university was on the way. From there I would proceed to the building to do what I had decided. Upon arriving at the university, I saw in the program that in the afternoon a priest was going to speak. I decided to stay and listen to him. Father, when you speak, you cannot imagine what goes on in the minds of the people who listen to you. Your words save lives! For God's sake, don't stop!

I confess that, when I read this letter, I was very moved, and that I have rarely been so moved in my life. In all my years as a priest, I have never had an experience as dramatic as this one. After that, this young man and I spoke frequently for several years. Fortunately, he overcame the depression he was in and the suicidal urges.

The theme of theology and the LGBTQ+ community, far from being merely an abstract issue, has a visceral and decisive impact on the lives of many people. Pope Francis greatly motivates us to take up this theme, as he teaches that the theologian must live on a frontier, assume the conflicts that affect everyone and, with his reflection, pour oil and wine on the wounds of men, like the good Samaritan of the Gospel.[1] He also challenges us by stating that "doctrine cannot be preserved without allowing it to develop, nor can it be tied to an interpretation that is rigid and immutable without demeaning the working of the Holy Spirit."[2]

Finally, the objective of this book is to encourage the pouring of oil and wine on human wounds and to collaborate for the progress of the doctrine. Our words can save lives, or they can destroy them. May they save them.

1

SEXUALITY AND THE JUDEO-CHRISTIAN TRADITION

The Judeo-Christian tradition is a set of ideas, values, practices, and institutions that has shaped peoples and civilizations in the East and West. It goes back to Jesus Christ and his apostles and disciples, who founded the Church and composed the Scriptures, incorporating the Hebrew Scriptures and rereading them from a new perspective. This tradition spans generations and millennia, always confronting and adapting to new contexts. It has a dialectic of conservation and change so that its contents remain intelligible and relevant. An important twentieth-century theologian, Yves Congar, said that the only way to say the same thing in a context that has changed is to say it differently.[1] Nothing is stranger to tradition than fixism[2] that refuses any change, like a fossil in a natural history museum. Tradition is not traditionalism. This is a misconception that leads to ruin because it destroys its vitality and dynamism. Like a river that receives tributaries from its watershed and becomes more abundant, the Judeo-Christian tradition crosses the centuries interacting with new cultures and contexts, where the Church must interpret the signs of the times in the light of the word of God. Only in this way can the message always be the Gospel, the good news, that gives meaning to life, heals wounds, and warms hearts, and is not a sterile anachronism. This tradition, originating from Israel, was inserted into the Greco-Roman world. In it, theology later developed along with its perspective on sexuality.

The word *sex* comes from the Latin *secare*, which means to divide, split, or intersect. Etymology itself suggests that sex carries the originality born of separation and the resulting approximation of a desire back to the origins. Sex is connected to embodiment. We are born from the conjugation of two bodies. We are aware of who we are in relation to the bodies of others and to other realities. The consciousness of being and existing presupposes the consciousness of being with others and coexisting. The body is the symbolic support of individuality. Races, various cultures, and subcultures imprint traces on people's bodies, as well as social classes and professions. Thus, the body of a handyman often has different traits from that of an office worker.

Sexuality permeates every person. It is a fundamental dimension of the human being. Even before freedom intervenes in the elaboration of a life project, sexuality determines a feminine or masculine way of being in the world. It is present in every cell of the human being and throughout life. Twenty-four hours a day, we are either men or women. Everything about us is sexed, but not everything is sexual. When it comes to sexual activity or behavior, it's usually about genitality—the part organically intended for pleasure and procreation. It is a privileged way of expressing sexuality that does not exhaust it. Sexuality is the being-man or being-woman while different from each other. Even apart from all genital activity, human beings are still totally sexed in everything they do and in everything they are.[3] These statements are commonly accepted, but questions arise when it comes to sexual diversity.

For a deeper understanding of the meaning of sexuality, it is necessary to relate it to spirituality. Our sexuality is structured from a body that is the basis of our biological, psychic-affective, social, and cosmic relationships, including the spiritual dimension. From a theological perspective, our bodies are temples of God and destined for the glory of the resurrection. Our sexuality is a privileged channel that connects human love and divine love. This spiritual dimension, an openness to transcendence, is not easily understood in a secular context. But the search for spiritual literature of various religious hues is symptomatic. It seems to indicate a saturation of merely biological and immediate pleasures. The search for the meaning of life and happiness requires something more, even from those who do not have a religious affiliation.[4]

THE ANCIENT CONTEXT

The surroundings of ancient Israel strongly affected its history, culture, and religion through the assimilation and its rejection of content and practices. Sexuality and marriage in neighboring cultures had archetypal figures of the father god and mother goddess, who were sources of life in the divine, human, and natural realms. Myths celebrated the marriage, union, and fertility of the divine couple, such as Baal and Anat. Thus, they deified sexuality and legitimized the marriage, intercourse, and fertility of each earthly couple. The rituals represented myths and established a concrete connection between the divine world and the earthly world. Consequently, they enabled men and women to share the divine action and effectiveness of this action. The sexual rituals would bless sexual intercourse and ensure that divine fertility was shared by plants, animals, and the wives of a man, for all these beings were important in the struggle for survival in those ancient cultures.[5]

The ancient Greco-Roman world greatly influenced the Judaism diaspora and Christianity, especially the Hellenic culture. The Jews outside Palestine, far more numerous than their Palestinian counterparts, translated the Scriptures into the Greek language. This is also the language of the New Testament, which has become a very important cultural component in the lives of Jews and Christians. Hellenic cosmology influenced the Judeo-Christian tradition with a strong contempt for the world and the human being, as will be seen later. In this cosmology, the sublunar world opposes the supralunar world—the lower bodies (*corpora inferiora*) to the celestial bodies (*corpora caelestia*). Below the earth, there is only hell. The earth occupies the lower and most vulgar part of the world, because among the four existing elements—water, earth, fire, and air—it consists of the least noble element. The exiled soul of the heavenly world is a prisoner on earth. The devaluation of nature is inseparable from the depreciation of time. Earthly things are vain because they are fleeting. The human being does not escape this contempt. Plutarch, leaning on Homer's *Iliad*, states: "Nothing is more miserable than a man among all that breathes and moves." This is a heritage of the Hellenic tradition.[6]

The concept of family and some of its characteristics were common in several Mediterranean peoples. The term family comes from the Latin *famulus*, which means domestic slave. This term is from ancient Rome, from the Latin tribes linked to *agriculture* and legalized *slavery*. Originally, a family was a set of slaves living under one roof. It was based on marriage and blood bonds, made up of spouses and their children. The dominance of man—husband, father, and lord—was undisputed. In Greco-Roman antiquity, at least among women and men of the elite, erotic intercourse could be sought with partners other than spouses. Concubinage, prostitution, and male relations with slaves were allowed and common. The phrase attributed to Demosthenes is famous: "Indeed, the *heteras* (prostitutes) we have them for pleasure, the concubines for the daily care of the body, but wives to have legitimate children and keep faithful custody of the house."[7]

Divorce was readily available in Greece and at the end of the Roman Empire. In both, it was legislated by the economic situation of divorced women. Abortion and infanticide were generally accepted as forms of birth control. Marriage was not a matter of love, which does not mean that conjugal love was always absent between spouses. Men were expected to marry to generate an heir, but for them, the greatest love resided in sexual or other intercourse with other men, because among them there was an equality that could never be achieved with a woman.[8]

The attitude of Greeks and Romans toward sexuality is largely due to their philosophers. The Greek dualism between body and soul, diminishing the body, led to a mistrust of sex and the disqualification of sexual pleasure. Plato and Aristotle regarded sexual pleasure as an inferior pleasure shared with other animals. Plato defended overcoming it in favor of the higher pleasures of good, beauty, and truth. Aristotle, in addressing it in general terms, advocated its moderation. The Stoic Musonius Rufus considers marriage a natural institution with two objectives: one is sexual intercourse and procreation, and the other is the communion of life between the spouses, which is the most important and praiseworthy of all human communions. Rufus and Seneca wondered about the purpose of sexual activity, seeking to order it rationally. The answer was procreation. Therefore, this activity was moral only when practiced for the sake of procreation. And later Stoics not only asserted that sexual activity was intended for procreation, but also that it should be restricted to marital boundaries. Sex outside marriage was immoral. Stoic philosophers not only limited it to "conjugal" relations but also limited the purpose of sexual relations to "procreation."[9]

THE JUDEO-CHRISTIAN TRADITION

There is a certain originality in the biblical revelation of love and sexuality that is clearly manifested in how the Jewish religion ruptures with the other surrounding religions. There is no mother goddess, no lover goddess, and no wife goddess. Even if Yahweh is named with the archetype of the father (cf. Exod 4:22–23; Deut 1:31; Hos 11:1; Isa 1:2), this name has nothing to do with the fertility myth, but with the way God relates to his people. The faith of Israel, like the Christian faith, refutes the existence of a mother goddess with the Father God. Myths and sexual rites have been excluded from their origins. In Israel, there is no hierogamy, marriage between gods, and sacred prostitution was forbidden with the death penalty (cf. Deut 22:1–19). Mythical sacralization of human sexuality is not admitted. This is the *via negativa* of the originality of biblical revelation.

There were also ritual prescriptions and sexual taboos. They were not linked to morality but to the ritualistic categories of pure and impure. Deep down, such detailed and strict prescriptions manifest a fear of sex, a kind of taboo. The motivations are not hygienic or aesthetic, but religious. As in other neighboring peoples of Israel and the Palestinian population, sexual phenomena were considered an impediment to the cultic relationship with God.[10] Menstruation and pathological flow make the woman and all people and objects touched by her unclean for seven days (Lev 15:19–23). Childbirth makes the woman impure for seven days in the case of giving birth to a boy, and fourteen days in the case of a girl. The woman was to remain at home for thirty-three days if a boy was born, forbidden to go to the sanctuary, and for sixty-six days if a girl was born (cf. Lev 12:1–6). Every seminal discharge makes the man unclean, and the conjugal act makes the husband and wife unclean until evening. They should purify themselves with a ritualized bath (cf. Lev 15:16–18).

With all this, conjugal love was introduced into the realm of the covenant. Prophets use the comparison of human marriage to explain God's relationship with his chosen people—the Lord is the husband, and the people are the wife. The drama of the human couple, of love and infidelity, of fruitfulness and unhappiness, is the best comparison to understand the drama of God's relationship with his people. Hosea, Jeremiah, Ezekiel, and Isaiah develop this theme with literary beauty and theological depth. When a couple of Israel lived their love, they knew that they were fulfilling the mystery of God's love for their people. The qualities of love, such as fidelity, surrender, and exclusivity, as well as its failures, especially infidelity, receive a new evaluation, that is, the religious appreciation of the history of salvation.[11]

The dignity of man and woman was affirmed, equally created in the image and likeness of God (cf. Gen 1 and 2), but male domination in a patriarchal regime was clear. The wife was the property of the husband or father, as was the house, the slave, the ox, and the donkey (cf. Exod 20:17). A father could sell his daughters as slaves (cf. Exod 21:7). Marriage was an agreement between householders, waiving the consent of the spouses. The man could have more than one wife, like the patriarch Jacob, and her function was to beget descendants for her husband's family. If the wife were widowed and childless, she would have to marry her brother-in-law to fulfill this function. It is the so-called levirate law (cf. Deut 25:5–10). Over time, marriage became monogamous.

Biblical teachings, however, are not homogeneous. There are different nuances. One of their literary genres, wisdom literature, was able to articulate the Jewish faith with the human wisdom of different cultures and proposed an ideal of love and sexuality with expressive richness and anthropological content. In it, notably, is the Song of Songs, which is a hymn to human love, where there is an unreserved affirmation of sexuality and human eroticism. According to some exegetical studies, this work is inspired by the courtesan literature of Egypt and reflects a certain humanism of the Solomonic era. For Edward Schillebeeckx,

> the work, which is possibly linked to a wedding feast, is not so much about conjugal love as about the physical beauty and sensual love of two young people. The same environment in which it was composed, the court during the season of ancient Israel kings, does not allow us to think of a prophetic tradition influence later, which painted the divine covenant in the guise of marriage....The Song thus constitutes a healthy counterweight to all other Old Testament lines of thought which regard marriage almost exclusively as a means of perpetuating the clan and the people. Probably to react against the rites of fertility, the Canticle does not exalt the glories of the large family but praises above all human love.[12]

The Song of Songs has always caused strangeness to the interpreters, in doubt about whether it is an ode to divine love or to human love. For many centuries, Christian commentators did not want to attribute erotic love a place in sacred writings, due to negative assumptions about sexuality. Therefore, they prudently and allegorically chose a spiritual meaning. The Song of Songs would deal with Yahweh's love for Israel, as well as God's love for the individual soul. But this book was included in the Hebrew canon before there was any suggestion of its allegorical interpretation. The faith of Israel did not see the profane nature of the book as an impediment to accepting it as Scripture. Theologian Karl Barth considers the Song of Songs as a "second Magna Carta" that develops the view of relationship proposed in the second chapter of Genesis, where equality between man and woman is observed. The Song of Songs may be an allegory of divine love but only in a secondary way. It can apply to spiritual love but in a derivative way. The first reality is human, erotic love, a love that makes every lover "faint with love" (2:5). This book does not remind us of the degradation of sexual desire and pleasure in Plato and Aristotle, for it is a celebration of human love and the sexual desire of lovers. Christian history has greatly "infused" the egalitarian sexual relationship between man and woman into a patriarchal system, institutionalized it within the boundaries of marriage and procreation, and followed Plato and Aristotle in their suspicion of sexual pleasure.[13]

With the coming of Jesus Christ, the revelation reaches its fullness, recognizing that "God is love" (1 John 4:8). Jesus is the living manifestation of the love of God the Father who loved the world so much (John 3:16) and sent his Spirit to the hearts of the faithful. Jesus did not determine a special form of marriage but demanded the fulfillment of the ideal of love existing "from the beginning" in the first human couple, of which the two become "one flesh." Until then, God did not demand it out of pedagogical condescension in view of the "hardness of heart." The teaching of Jesus aims to bring to full realization the reality of love as it is given by the Creator. The account of the Gospels (see Mark 10:1–12; Matt 19:3–12) should not be interpreted as a law but as a prophetic proclamation of the profound reality of conjugal love, as well as the possibility of bringing it to this fullness within the Christian faith.[14]

This ideal has even greater strength in the context of the patriarchal society of Jesus's time. The woman who no longer found "favor in his eyes" (of her husband) could be dismissed by means of an act of divorce (cf. Deut 24:1). Only the husband could take the initiative. And not finding grace in her husband's eyes was a concept that divided the rabbis in their interpretation of the Law of Moses. Some restricted this clause only to adultery. Others expanded it to the most futile motives: if the woman had ceased to be beautiful, if she let the food burn, had warts, or bad breath. Divorce greatly weakened the woman in a society where she depended on the man. The dismissed woman was exposed to misery, begging, and prostitution. Such was the situation of the widows who had no husband nor state pension, and who had difficulty surviving. That is why prophets preached defending the orphan, the foreigner, and the widow, who were the most vulnerable social segments, exposed to misery and oppression.

The theologian Bernhard Häring, wishing to give an answer to the situation of the divorced, made an important consideration of the indissolubility of marriage understood as precept. According to him, there are two types of precept: the *goal* precept and the *limit* precept. The goal precept is ideal, and the limit precept is the law. Indissoluble marriage is the gospel, the good news that is on the level of grace and is the gift of God. It is a goal precept, an ideal that not everyone is able to achieve. It is something that cannot be accomplished by law, whether civil or canonical.[15] It is, therefore, necessary to seek pastoral ways to deal with this situation, as Pope Francis did in *Amoris Laetitia*, his exhortation to the synod of bishops on the family.

Besides Jesus, Paul the apostle is another fundamental reference of the Judeo-Christian tradition. Jesus preached the closeness of the kingdom or reign of God (cf. Mark 1:15). Paul was convinced that "the present form of this world is passing away" (1 Cor 7:31). The interpretation of any New Testament statement regarding sexuality must take this assumption into account. Paul challenges the Ascetics and Gnostics who determined celibacy for all Christians, saying that marriage is good yet only to avoid sexual sins. He affirms the equality between men and women in marriage and the reciprocal duty: "For the wife does not have authority over her own body, but the husband does; likewise the husband does not have authority over his own body, but the wife does" (1 Cor 7:4).

The Pauline writings, however, include letters written by his disciples after the apostle's death. These letters bear the name of Paul by a process of literary paternity that is common in the Bible, just as other texts are attributed to Moses, David, or Solomon without them necessarily being the authors. In the post-Pauline letters, there is a clear subordination of the wife to the husband: "For the husband is the head of the wife just as Christ is the head of the church" (Eph 5:23). But this "just as" makes a big difference. The command of a Christian husband over his wife should have as its reference the command of Christ over the Church. And the way Christ exercises this authority leaves no doubt: "For the Son of Man came not to be served but to serve, and to give his life a ransom for many" (Mark 10:45). *Diakonia* (service) is the Christian way of exercising authority. Therefore, conjugal authority modeled on Christ does not mean controlling, giving orders, or making unreasonable demands, and reducing the other person to the slavery of whims. It means service for the sake of love.[16]

The New Testament values the Genesis doctrine of equality, attraction, and complementarity of the sexes. There is a forceful statement in the Letter of Paul to the Galatians: "As many of you as were baptized into Christ have clothed yourselves with Christ. There is no longer Jew or Greek, there is no longer slave or free, there is no longer male and female; for all of you are one in Christ Jesus" (Gal 3:27–28). This statement does not suppress sexual reality but must be understood from a religious perspective. It is Christ who gives value to the human being, not sex, nationality, or social class. Among the baptized who are clothed with Christ, the difference between man and woman loses its importance and its disaggregating force. It can be said that there are two views about women in the Bible: the submissive and the egalitarian. The two need to be distinguished in any dialogue that includes the Bible, Christian tradition, and contemporary human experience.[17]

In the Christian world, male domination in marriage has gone through many centuries without dispute. In 1880, Pope Leo XIII stated: "The husband is the chief of the family and the head of the wife. The woman, because she is the flesh of his flesh, and bone of his bone, must be subject to her husband and obey him; not, indeed, as a servant, but as a companion." The order of love—as St. Augustine calls it—flourishes by consolidating domestic society with the bond of charity. This order implies the superiority of the husband over the wife and children, and the woman's prompt subjection and obedience. If the man is the head, the woman is the heart, as Pope Pius XI taught. If he has the primacy of government, she must take care of love. The woman's subjection to her husband may vary according to the diversity of people, times, and places. And even if the man lacks his duty in the direction of the family, it is up to the woman to provide it. But in no time and place is it lawful to subvert or harm this essential structure of the family and its law established by God.[18]

The Christian revelation on human love brings a novelty—the discovery of virginity. Human love can be lived in a completely new way. The Old Testament did not know the ideal of virginity. On the contrary, virginity was a countervalue. The celibacy of Jeremiah (ch. 16) symbolizes the futility of Israel and the calamity of the times that prevent the marriage. The daughter of Jephthah, before being sacrificed, grieves not for having to die, but for dying without having married and borne children (Judg 11:40). With the coming of Christ, the concept and reality of virginal love arise. The celibate Christ announces and realizes the new times in which the virginal dimension of human love, with its spiritual fruitfulness, also acquires meaning. The New Testament exposes and completes the mystery of Christian virginity, initiated in the person of Jesus, in the Gospels (cf. Matt 19:10–12; 22:30; Luke 14:26) and in the Pauline writings (e.g., 1 Cor 7).

Both conjugal and virginal love have the mystery of Christ's love for the Church as their source. This mystery cannot be translated into Christian life only in the institution of marriage or in the virginal state; it needs both. The Christians of Corinth, faced with the newness of Christian times, wanted to put an end to marriages. Paul, however, reminds them of their validity, for even if "the present form of this world is passing away" (1 Cor 7:31), marriage will last until the return of Christ. But marriage must be "in the Lord" (1 Cor 7:39), sharing in the surpassing fullness of his mystery. Sexuality also has an eschatological dimension, related to the ultimate destiny of the human being, as it makes the kingdom of God more present by awakening affection, producing justice, and creating committed love.[19]

In the early Church, there was a desire to regulate sexual life. The doctrine on the sins of sexuality, however, was not of primary importance in the New Testament. This teaching appears frequently in the moral literary genre of catalogs of vices and virtues, coming from postbiblical Judaism with the influence of the Hellenistic environment. In the catalogs of vices (cf. Rom 1:29–31; 13:13; 1 Cor 5:10–11; 6:9–10; 2 Cor 12:20–21; Gal 5:19–21; Eph 4:31; 5:3–5; Col 3:5–8; 1:9–10; 2 Tim 3:2–4), idolatry appears frequently in the foreground, often associated with sexual impurity and disorder. The main sexual sins that the New Testament enumerates are fornication and adultery. The term used for fornication, *porneia*, applies to religious infidelity (cf. Rev 17—19) and appears in the clause on divorce (cf. Matt 5:32; 19:9). But in classical Greek, it means lust: sexual intercourse between man and woman outside marriage, which can be strict fornication (cf. 1 Cor 6:12–20), adultery (cf. 1 Cor 7:2), or incest (cf. 1 Cor 5:1).

Even with these catalogs of vices and virtues, the New Testament does not provide any casuistry of sexual morality, nor does it indicate concrete guidelines for each of the situations of sexual behavior.[20] According to the late Carlo Maria Martini, a biblical scholar, cardinal, and archbishop emeritus of Milan, the Church can and must be guided by the Bible. But the Bible is sober in statements about sexuality. In relation to adultery, it draws a clear line of conduct: it is absolutely forbidden to destroy another's marriage. And it is also very clear when it comes to violence against women. It is forbidden. Jesus places children and all who need protection at the center. How we treat children reveals the degree of humanity reached by society. In addition to these clear lines taught by the Bible, Christians are left to their own responsibility and to the discernment of spirits.[21] In this discernment, it is necessary to recognize and distinguish the various inner movements and ideas that affect the freedom of the person. What comes from God and leads to him must be welcomed. What comes from evil and moves away from God must be avoided.

There are testimonies of sexual life regulation in the first centuries of the Church. Already in the second century, Justin responds to Roman accusations about the sexual immorality of Christians in his *Apology*. He states: "We either marry from the beginning for the sole purpose of bearing children or renounce marriage, remaining absolutely chaste."[22] Clement of Alexandria, in turn, goes further, saying that the sole purpose of sexual intercourse is to bear children and that any other purpose must be excluded: "A man who marries to procreate children must exercise continence, so that he will not desire his wife whom he must love, and so that he can raise children with chastity and moderate will. For we are not children of desire, but of will." Origen, also from Alexandria, argues that the man who has sexual relations only with his wife, "and with her only at certain legitimate times and only for his children," is truly circumcised. In the fourth century another Alexandrine, Athanasius, states that "blessed is the man who, in his youth, is united in marriage for the procreation of children," but also that "there are two ways of life, one inferior and vulgar, namely marriage; and another, angelic and supreme above all, namely virginity."[23]

The Gnostics, the Encratites ("self-controlled"), who condemned marriage, and the Manicheans left their marks. Christian doctrine, even the official one, has not been free from a prevalence of virginity and continence over marriage, leading to a certain dangerous imbalance in relation to the teaching of Scripture. Stoicism is at the root of the unilateral view of sexuality focused exclusively on procreation. Even if Christian authors of the past cited abundantly the primordial biblical commandment "Be fruitful and multiply" (Gen 1:28), the context of the Bible brings a broader view of sexuality. The Pauline teaching on virginity and marriage does not insist on the relationship between sexuality and procreation. The dull insistence on justifying the sexual act solely for the procreative purpose proceeds largely from Stoicism. Rufus had a great influence on Christian thought. This Latin author also preserves fragments in Greek, in which he opposes contraception and declares it illegitimate to seek only pleasure in marriage, except for procreation.

The Greek Christian notion of the nature of sexuality, like that of Stoic philosophers, is assimilated by Latin Christians. In the early fourth century, it is well expressed by the North African Lactantius:

> Just as God gave us the eyes, not to contemplate and enjoy pleasure, but so that through them we see the acts that affect the vital needs, so the genital part of the body is not given to us, as its name teaches, for anything but producing offspring. To this divine law, we must obey with great devotion.[24]

This teaching was commonly accepted and has spanned centuries. By its very nature, sexual intercourse is intended to bear children. Any other use is immoral, for it contradicts this nature that is divine law. And every sexual intercourse in which conception is impossible is equally immoral. The legality of the sexual act without immediate procreation does not appear as a common doctrine until the seventeenth century. The emergence of other reasons that justified the conjugal act was slow and painful.[25]

An author who has profoundly marked Western culture is Saint Augustine, bishop of Hippo. On marriage, he says: "The good of marriage, which even the Lord in the Gospel has confirmed...seems to be not only the procreation of children but also the natural companionship/friendship [*societas*] between the sexes. Otherwise, we could not speak of marriage among the elderly."[26] Regarding sexual intercourse, he states that it is only good when it is intended for the generation of children, following the position of the Stoics and the Alexandrians. After the fall of Adam, any other use, even between couples in marriage, is at least a venial sin. A venial sin is committed when, in a light matter, the measure prescribed by the moral law is not observed or when, in a grave matter, one disobeys the moral law, but without full knowledge or without full consent. For the bishop of Hippo, "conjugal sexual intercourse for the sake of offspring is not sinful. But sexual intercourse, even with one's own partner, to satisfy concupiscence [disordered desire] is a venial sin."[27]

According to Augustine, before Adam's fall and expulsion from paradise, "man, then, would have sown the seed, and the woman received it, as need required, the generative organs being moved by the will, not excited by lust." The human being would dominate these organs as he dominates the feet, hands, fingers, and lungs, being able to breathe, exhale, speak, sing, or shout. "And therefore man himself also might very well have enjoyed absolute power over his members had he not forfeited it by his disobedience."[28] The human being would have control of his sexual activity, with a will governed by reason and not dragged by lust. But "since man placed in honor fell, he has become like the beasts, and generates as they do, though the little spark of reason, which was the image of God in him, has not been quite quenched."[29] Therefore, irrational animality predominates in human sexual activity and procreation, even if some reason remains.

The doctrine of original sin, based on the first chapters of the Bible, profoundly marked Christian thought, including the field of sexuality. To this day, it is taught that at the beginning of human history, there was a man and a woman created in a state of holiness, dispensed from death, and living in harmony with the surrounding nature,[30] in an environment and situation traditionally called earthly paradise. The sin committed by the first human couple in paradise is passed on to everyone else by the generation, along with its consequences, becoming the sin proper to every human being. Today there are those who argue that the enormity attributed to the first offense should be reconsidered, as well as the death sentence and the resulting hereditary guilt. It would be better to speak of the "sin of the world" that Jesus comes to remove, according to the Gospel of John (1:29), to mean that we are all born into a world in which sin already exists. A world in which wickedness, pride, willpower, and concupiscence have accumulated since the beginning of humanity.[31]

Even though, today, many Christians reconsider the biblical account and such doctrine, until the eighteenth century, the concept of original sin with its consequences was the most widely accepted explanation for most of the evils that afflicted humanity. The divine punishment that punished Adam and his descendants was present not only in the death of every person, but also in natural catastrophes, fulfilling the Scriptures: "cursed is the ground because of you… / you are dust, / and to dust you shall return" (Gen 3:17–19). This past pessimistic view of the world, matter, body, sex, and procreation is quite remarkable.

The impurity of sex, even when it is lawful, relates to the contempt of the world and humanity, derived from Hellenism that developed in the Judeo-Christian tradition. The Book of Ecclesiastes laments the vanity of vanities (*vanitas vanitatum*), for "all was vanity and a chasing after wind, and there was nothing to be gained under the sun" (Eccl 2:11). Paul says that "we know that while we are at home in the body we are away from the Lord" (2 Cor 5:6). This is an echo of the Platonic idea of the body as a prison of the soul. The word "world" in the Gospels is ambiguous: sometimes it refers to the field where weeds and wheat grow together, the children of the kingdom and the children of the evil one (cf. Matt 13:38); sometimes it refers to the creation and the human being loved by God, who loved them to the point of giving his only son (cf. John 3:16); and sometimes it refers to those who hate Christ and his disciples (John 15:18). Often, this last sense of "world" prevailed, laden with pessimism and mistrust.

In Christian antiquity, monasticism develops as a *fuga mundi*, an escape from the world, an ideal of celibate Christian life and withdrawal from ordinary conviviality. Monks become the successors of martyrs as a model of giving their lives for the love of Christ and the Gospel. According to the eleventh-century monk Peter Damian, the secular world is essentially lustful. To leave the secular environment and enter a monastery is to "leave Sodom." A secular society and a corrupt society are synonymous, and it is difficult to achieve salvation. There is a depreciation of all earthly tasks and a suspicion cast also on priests who are not monks, because "close to the secular and mixed with them due to their geographic neighborhood, the majority no longer distinguish themselves from their way of living and their unruly customs."[32]

For many centuries in Christendom, clergy are almost the only ones to express themselves in writing. The ideal Christian was the monk. The calendar of saints admitted almost only bishops, monks, and religious men from congregations. Eventually, some prematurely widowed princesses spent the rest of their lives in penance and assistance to the poor. Saint Bernard of Clairvaux compares the world to a vast sea that must be crossed to achieve salvation. The monks cross through a bridge and do not get wet. The secular clergy makes use of the boat of Peter. Married people, unfortunately, must swim and many drown on the way. Some pious lay people, unable to become monks, strived to approach the monastic life. Saint Louis, King of France, practiced numerous mortifications and recited the liturgy of the hours, rising at dawn for morning prayer. Many lay people, at the end of their lives, asked to be buried dressed in monastic habit.[33]

One of the greatest Christian exponents of contempt of the world and of humanity is Cardinal Lothar of Segni, future Pope Innocent III (1198–1216). He is the author of a work on the poverty of the human condition with a wide diffusion. Forty-seven editions of the work are known, of which 672 manuscripts are preserved to this day. For Segni, "man is formed of dust, mud, ash and that which is most vile, of filthy sperm....He was born for work, for fear, for pain and, what is worse, for death." Quoting the Psalm that says "Indeed, I was born guilty, / a sinner when my mother conceived me " (51:5), he comments:

> Who in fact ignores that conjugal coupling never occurs without the itching of the flesh, the fermentation of desire, and the odor of lust? Thus, all offspring, by their own conception, are corrupted, tainted, and addicted, since the seed transmits to the soul that is infused with the stain of sin, the mark of guilt, the dirt of iniquity. In the same way, a liquid becomes corrupted if it is poured into a polluted vessel and, touching what is polluted, is polluted by contact.[34]

It is worth considering the underlying anthropology. Before the nineteenth century, the egg cell, or ovum, was unknown. It was believed that in the ejaculation of men was contained the entire human being in miniature, a homunculus, that soon received from God the immortal soul. Hence the name "semen," with the same root as a seed. This homunculus must be placed in the womb of the woman as the seed is deposited in the earth. As original sin is transmitted to other human beings by generation, it is through semen that this transmission takes place. Coming from the itch of the flesh, the libido and lust are the "filthy sperm" that impregnates the newly generated soul with the stain of sin, the mark of guilt, and the dirt of iniquity.

This contempt of the world and of humanity can also be seen in another even more widespread work: *The Imitation of Christ*, by Thomas à Kempis, published in the fifteenth century. Its circulation is only surpassed by the Bible. Kempis states:

> Truly to know and despise self is the best and most perfect counsel....All men are frail, but you must admit that none is more frail than yourself....Living on earth is truly a misery. The more a man desires spiritual life, the more bitter the present becomes to him, because he understands better and sees more clearly the defects, the corruption of human nature....But woe to those who know not their own misery, and greater woe to those who love this miserable and corruptible life.[35]

Christian spirituality associated self-worth with suffering and pain as a path of sanctification. The Dominican friar Luis de Granada, the author of the famous *The Sinner's Guide* (1556–1557), said that where the sufferings of the world are found, there are the favors of heaven, and where there is the resistance of nature there is the help of grace, more powerful than nature. But it is necessary to treat the body with rigor and hardness. The dead meat is preserved with salt and myrrh, which is very bitter, otherwise, it spoils and fills with worms. So too the body is corrupted and filled with vices if it is treated with solicitudes and delicacies.[36] This friar advocates, in short, the "holy hatred of oneself" and the mortification of all passions, which he calls sensory appetite. This is the lowest part of our soul, which makes us more animal-like.[37]

Many teachings and attitudes of the Church regarding sexuality are found in manuals of the sacrament of penance. This penitential literature developed between the sixth and twelfth centuries, and contributed to a moral perspective that focuses on individual acts, considering moral life as a matter of avoiding sin, and turning moral reflection into an analysis of sin in its many forms. In the thirteenth century, however, Scholasticism, on one level, valued personal relationships and equality between husband and wife. Bonaventure called friendship between spouses the sacrament of the relationship between God and the soul. Mutual love between spouses is not an exclusively modern concern.[38]

In the modern age, starting in the sixteenth century, sexual morality is exposed in two ways: in the treatise on the sixth and ninth commandments, and in the treatise on marriage. In the catechetical formula, the sixth commandment is not to sin against chastity. Originally, it is "you shall not commit adultery" (Exod 20:14), but the Christian doctrine incorporated within it other biblical teachings concerning sexuality. Chastity comes from the Latin *castus*: that which adjusts, conforms to laws or rules, what is correct. The ninth commandment is not to covet another's wife (Exod 20:17). The theologians of Salamanca sought to prove that all sexual morality is contained explicitly in these two commandments of the Decalogue. As much as we want to broaden the horizon of the Decalogue, it is difficult to reach the entire field of sexual morality through its formulations.

Chastity, as a positive aspect of sexuality, will be considered by the manuals of casuistic morality from a biological and genital conception of sexuality. Lust, the vice opposed to it, had the same reductionist leveling. Sexual sin is defined from this same perspective, situated in the "action of the genitals" or in the misuse of the "seminal liquid." The notion of pleasure is mixed with the adhesions of a Neoplatonic mentality. Sometimes they relate it to original sin, the effects of which include the depravity of all human pleasure and, more specifically, sexual pleasure.[39] This reality is called "lust," a disordered appetite for dishonest pleasures contrary to reason, the result of human beings' natural propensity to do evil as a consequence of original sin.

The sexual relationship between married people, even if licit and correct, contained a certain impurity. In the sixteenth century, the Catechism of the Council of Trent established that, in order to receive the Eucharist, a couple should temporarily abstain from sex: "Such a sublime Sacrament also requires the dignity that married people to abstain for a few days, like David who, before receiving the offering loaves from the priest, assured that he and his soldiers, for three days, were far from their wives (1 Sam 21:5)" (Cat. Romano, II, IV, §54). Parish priests must teach the faithful to refrain from conjugal relations from time to time, for the sake of their prayers and supplications to God. This must happen not only at least three days before receiving the Eucharist but also during the time when the "holy fast of Lent" is observed, according to the prescriptions left by the holy priests (Cat. Romano, II, VIII, §34).

One can compare the influence of Hellenic dualism and Neoplatonism on the sexual doctrine of the fathers of the Church and on the history of Christian morality. This influence is manifested through derogatory metaphysics of matter, as well as a perspective of abstaining from sexual activity, even in marriage. The Encratites' influence can be observed: in prohibitions, as above, that today seem scandalous; in negative conceptions of the conjugal act as "not without inconvenience" or "permissible, but scabrous"; in pessimism toward all that is sexual; in the conception of the virtue of chastity with a strong emphasis on restriction and abstention; and in asceticism as a means of finding a purer life dedicated to contemplation. Only at the beginning of the twentieth century did moralists accept the permissibility of the pursuit of moderate pleasure among spouses outside the conjugal act.[40]

The pessimism toward all that is sexual is well exemplified in the memoirs of Marc Oraison, a Catholic priest who wrote about sexuality and had problems with religious authority. In 1955, his book on Christian life and problems of sexuality, the result of his doctoral thesis, was included in the Index of Forbidden Books, an instrument of control created at the time of the Counter-Reformation in the sixteenth century, which lasted until the Second Vatican Council (1962–1965). Before this decision, he was called by the Holy Office, the current Dicastery for the Doctrine of the Faith, and accounted for the meeting he had:

> The happening was grand and triumphant for employing a word of conciliation. I was alone, lost in a large, profusely decorated hall, sitting on a chair surrounded by two huge armchairs, one on the left and one on the right. In each armchair a cardinal: Pizardo, supreme head of the Holy Office, after the pope, and Ottaviani, his deputy. The first began to speak, and some of his phrases still resonate in my ears. This was the overall idea: my book was pernicious

> and "disturbed customs"; it endangered morale. For a good education about sexuality, nothing better than fear of hell and a starch-based diet. As for the future priests, he told me verbatim: "For purity in seminaries there is nothing like terror, spaghetti, and green beans." I was devastated.[41]

Despite the pessimism on sexuality, there have been important changes in the field of marriage and the family. In the twelfth century, a compilation of ecclesiastical law appeared in Western Christianity. A novelty unprecedented in history is introduced: the consent of the couple as a necessary condition for the validity of marriages. Consent could be given both in the future and in the present. When given in the future, it was called the nuptial pact, and the process was known as *sponsalia* or spousals. The members of the couple became spouses. When consent was given in the present, it was called marriage, and the process was known as *nuptialia* or nuptials. The members of the couple became engaged. The first sexual intercourse between the spouses usually took place after the marriage pact. Very often, especially in the countryside, marriage in the Church was performed when the woman became pregnant, sometimes near the end of pregnancy. In a society where procreation was central to marriage, sexual intercourse tested the fertility that was expected.

This practice only changed after the Council of Trent. To prohibit clandestine marriage, no one else could claim that marriage was effective in the nuptial pact. It could only be effective in a public religious ceremony called marriage. The nuptial pact lost its public character and became an internal family issue, called engagement, a prelude to marriage that did not confer matrimonial rights on its members, including sexual intercourse. An engaged couple could never be confused with a married couple who had celebrated the marriage.[42]

Among the goals of marriage, procreation always had primacy. In 1917, the Code of Canon Law outlined these objectives: "The primary end of marriages is procreation and the education of offspring; their secondary end is mutual assistance and the remedy for concupiscence" (Can 1013,1). But gradually a personalized understanding of marriage is introduced, expressed in this encyclical of Pius XI:

> This mutual molding of husband and wife, this determined effort to perfect each other, can in a very real sense, as the

> Roman Catechism teaches, be said to be the chief reason and purpose of matrimony, provided matrimony be looked at not in the restricted sense as instituted for the proper conception and education of the child, but more widely as the blending of life as a whole and the mutual interchange and sharing thereof.[43]

In the middle of the twentieth century, biblical studies advanced beyond the literal meaning of Scripture, leading to consequences in theology and morals. Pius XII teaches that there are "literary genres" in the Bible. What the sacred authors express is not as clear as in the writers of our time, says the pope. Their meaning cannot be determined only by the rules of grammar and philology, but also by the broader context of ancient Eastern times. The current interpreter must make use of history, archaeology, ethnology, and other sciences to examine and clearly distinguish which literary genres the writers of those remote times employed. With a correct concept of biblical inspiration, it should not be surprising that, in the sacred authors, as well as in their contemporaries, there are certain ways of exposing and telling, certain idiomatic particularities, especially of the Semitic languages, certain approximative or hyperbolic expressions, perhaps paradoxical, that serve to engrave things more firmly in memory. None of the ways of speaking of the ancients, especially among the Orientals, is incompatible with Scripture, since the adopted genre does not repudiate the holiness and truth of God.[44]

The questions of sexuality, family, and bioethics, as well as social issues, have as an indispensable theoretical reference the so-called natural law, very present in the teaching of the Catholic Church and in theology. In the Bible, the world is a divine creation, made according to the Creator's reason (*logos*), to manifest his wisdom (cf. John 1:1–3). There is supposed to be in creation a rationality that can be known by human beings and guide their action. There is also a law inscribed in the human heart that guides its ethical judgments, according to the apostle Paul (cf. Rom 2:12–16). As Pope Benedict XVI rightly sums up, the human being has received precious gifts from the Creator, such as the body itself, reason, freedom, and conscience, and there is also everything that philosophical tradition calls natural law. Every human being with awareness and responsibility experiences an inner call to do good and avoid evil. All the other precepts of natural law are based on this principle. Listening to the word of God leads first and foremost to appreciate the need to live according to this law inscribed in the heart. And Jesus Christ, logos, or incarnate word, gives to humanity the new law of the Gospel, which assumes and fulfills in a sublime way the natural law. This new law gives humanity participation in the divine life through grace and the ability to overcome selfishness.[45]

The precepts of the natural law, therefore, must be compatible with the divine Revelation, for both come from the same creator and redeemer God. Associated with natural law is the language of creation. God, creating and preserving all things by the word, offers humanity a permanent witness of himself in creation (*Dei Verbum* 3). As the mystery of Christ is at the center of divine revelation, it must be recognized that creation itself is also an essential part of a symphony of different voices in which the one word is expressed. Creation is compared to a book: *Liber Naturae* (Book of Nature). It is born of *logos* and brings the indestructible sign of creative reason that regulates and guides it. This certainty is expressed in the Psalms: "By the word of the LORD the heavens were made, and all their host by the breath of his mouth" (Ps 33:6). The Book of Nature is one and indivisible, whether it is about the environment or human life and its integral development.[46]

Natural law is like the source from which fundamental human rights and ethical imperatives spring. It is the bulwark against the will of power and the deceptions of ideological manipulation. Scientists have an important contribution to make. In addition to the ability to dominate nature, they can help to understand the responsibility of humans for their fellow human beings and the nature entrusted to them. Thus, it is possible to develop a "fruitful dialogue between believers and non-believers; between theologians, philosophers, jurists and scientists." This fruitful dialogue also offers the legislator valuable material for personal and collective life.[47]

The Church recognizes, however, that the expression of natural law is the source of numerous misunderstandings today. Sometimes, it simply refers to a resigned submission to the physical and biological laws of nature, when human beings seek, and rightly so, to dominate and direct these determinisms for their own good. Sometimes this law is presented as a given objective that imposes itself from outside the personal consciousness, regardless of what reason itself and subjectivity elaborate. It can be suspected of introducing an unbearable form of heteronomy into the dignity of the free human person. At other times, too, throughout its history, Christian theology very easily justified anthropological positions with natural law that were then conditioned by historical and cultural context. Today, it is appropriate to propose this doctrine in terms that better manifest the personal and existential dimensions of moral life. Natural law should not be presented as a list of definitive and immutable precepts, or as a set of rules already constituted that is imposed before the subject. This law is the foundation of a universal ethic, a source of objective inspiration for the subject's decision-making process, which is eminently personal.[48]

Catholic moral tradition has always recognized two heuristic principles for the discovery and understanding of its contents: human nature, studied by various types of human knowledge, and the word of God, pronounced in the Bible, transmitted by Christian tradition, and welcomed by faith. Regarding sexuality, Bernhard Häring noted: "We can calmly say that the Catholic Church, under the guidance of the magisterium, has always preserved the essence of the biblical message on sexuality, even admitting that the partial dissonances were deeper."[49]

THE SECOND VATICAN COUNCIL (1962–1965) AND THE PRESENT

Various values of modern society were assimilated by the Catholic Church at the Second Vatican Council that stated in the document, *Gaudium et Spes*, that "the joys and the hopes, the griefs and the anxieties of the men of this age, especially those who are poor or in any way afflicted, these are the joys and hopes, the griefs and anxieties of the followers of Christ. Indeed, nothing genuinely human fails to raise an echo in their hearts....That is why this community realizes that it is truly linked with mankind and its history by the deepest of bonds" (GS 1). Thus, this council breaks with the contempt of the world, of humanity, and with the *fuga mundi* that prevailed for so many centuries in the history of Christianity. The council legitimized the separation between church and state—a reality already consolidated in many countries—and the autonomy of science.

The Church's intimate connection with humanity and its history impels it to evangelize in a way adapted to the reality of people. There must be a permanent exchange between the Church and the different cultures. The Church recognizes that it needs the help of connoisseurs from various institutions and disciplines, whether they are believers or not. The faithful need to know how to listen and interpret the various languages or signs of the times, especially pastors and theologians, to evaluate them adequately in the light of the word of God, so that the divine truth is more closely perceived, presented conveniently (GS 4 and 44). Correct evangelization, therefore, is a two-way road of exchange between the Church and contemporary cultures.

In addition to attention to the signs of the times, the council encourages biblical studies that advance beyond the literal meaning of Scripture, on the path opened by Pius XII. *Dei Verbum* noted that divine revelation is expressed in various ways. The reader should seek the meaning that the sacred authors in certain circumstances, according to the conditions of their time and their culture, intended to express themselves using the literary genres used in the past (DV 12). In pastoral activity, in turn, theological principles are not enough, but the aid of profane sciences, especially psychology and sociology, is also needed to lead the faithful to a purer and more adult life of faith (GS 62).

In the council, the profound appreciation for the freedom of conscience of the human person is evident, associated with the duty to seek the truth. This freedom is the right of a person to act according to the right norm of their conscience, and the duty not to act against it. The conscience is the "tabernacle of the person," where God is present and manifested. By fidelity to the voice of conscience, Christians are united to other humans in the duty to seek the truth and to solve in it the moral problems that arise in individual and social life (GS 16). No external word replaces the reflection and judgment of one's conscience. Years later, the *Catechism of the Catholic Church* deepens this teaching and quotes St. John Henry Cardinal Newman, an important theologian of the nineteenth century: "Conscience is the aboriginal Vicar of Christ."[50] It is the one that first represents Christ for the faithful. Secular tasks and activities correspond to the laity as their own, though not exclusively. It is up to their previously well-formed consciousness to imprint the divine law on the life of the earthly city. From priests, the laity must expect spiritual light and nourishment. But "let the layman not imagine that his pastors are always such experts, that to every problem which arises, however complicated, they can readily give him a concrete solution, or even that such is their mission" (GS 43).

Faced with this freedom and autonomy of the faithful, recipients of Christ's message and belonging to different nations, races, and cultures, the Church seeks to be a sign of fraternity that makes dialogue possible and strengthens a sincere dialogue. This requires the recognition of all legitimate diversity and the promotion, in the Church itself, of mutual esteem, respect, and harmony to establish an evermore fruitful dialogue among those who form the people of God. The council wants that which unites the faithful to each other to become much stronger than what divides them, and urges: "Unity in what is necessary; freedom in what is unsettled, and charity in any case" (GS 92).

Regarding marriage and the family, it is affirmed that the intimate community of life and conjugal love has its foundation in the Creator and is endowed with its laws. It is instituted through the marriage covenant between man and woman, by irrevocable personal consent. Authentic conjugal love is assumed in divine love, directed, and enriched by the redemptive power of Christ and the action of the Church in favor of salvation, so that spouses may walk effectively to God, and be helped and strengthened in their sublime paternal and maternal mission. The Christian family, born of a marriage that is the image and participation of the covenant of love between Christ and the Church, manifests the living presence of the Savior in the world and the authentic nature of the Church, through the love of spouses, through their generous fruitfulness, unity and fidelity, and the kind cooperation of all its members (GS 48).

This love has its expression and fulfillment in the proper act of marriage, the sexual act. The acts by which spouses unite in intimacy and purity are honest and worthy. Performed in an authentic human way, they express and nourish the mutual surrender by which the spouses enrich each other in joy and gratitude (GS 49). Therefore, it is no longer perceived as an itch of the flesh, the fermentation of desire, and the smell of lust that also corrupts, stains, and addicts all offspring, and that should temporarily remove the couple from the sacrament of the Eucharist.

For the council, Christian spouses give glory to the Creator and walk toward perfection in Christ when they procreate with generous, human, and Christian responsibility. There is a special appreciation for those who, by mutual agreement, with prudence and greatness of mind, educate a large offspring. At the same time, the value of marriages where it is not possible to have descendants is recognized. Even if there are no children, so often ardently desired, marriage retains its value and indissolubility as a community and communion of all life (GS 50).

The hierarchy of the purpose of marriage in the 1917 canonical code was rejected, and the term "contract" was replaced by the biblical word "covenant" (*foedus*). This has the same legal results as a contract but places marriage in a biblical, theological, and interpersonal context, and does not have an exclusively juridical connotation. Covenant suggests a connection with the eternal covenants between God and Israel, and between Christ and the Church. The previous model of marriage was a procreative institution in which the act of sexual intercourse was primarily geared toward this purpose. The postconciliar model is an interpersonal union, in which sexual intercourse is primarily a unitive action. Protestant theologian Karl Barth once lamented that the traditional Christian doctrine of marriage, both Catholic and Protestant, placed it in juridical and nontheological categories. The Catholic Church corrected this imbalance with the council.[51]

The patriarchal model of the family, with male dominance, decayed worldwide throughout the twentieth century. The Universal Declaration of Human Rights, promulgated by the United Nations in 1948, established the free consent of spouses in the contract of marriage, and the equality of their rights in this union (Art. XVI). With the pontificate of John XXIII, the Catholic Church considers the U.N. declaration an act of the highest relevance and appreciates the entry of women into public life, as well as their claim of parity and rights with men.[52]

Thus, from Trent to Vatican II important changes were consolidated concerning marriage. Sexual relations between spouses are pure and honest, and no longer temporarily remove them from the Eucharist. The head of marriage is equally divided between man and woman, as occurs in the civil legislation of many countries, including Brazil. At the legal level, there is no longer male dominance over women. The idea of a marriage contract is replaced by the idea of a covenant, with its interpersonal and theological components. And the marriage purposes are no longer hierarchical but have the same value.

The regulation of births, in turn, generated such controversy in Vatican II that it was chosen not to have a pronouncement in this regard. The solution found was to refer the question to a commission subordinate to the pope to study it for a later decision of the pontiff (GS 51, note 14). Until then, there was in the Christian tradition a strong primacy of procreation in conjugal life and sexual intercourse. However, in 1880, the Roman Curia asserted that sexual intercourse is lawful in the days when conception is most difficult. This use of infertile periods may be suggested to spouses to ward off the "detestable crime of onanism," which is coitus interrupted for birth control purposes.[53] Sexual abstinence in fertile periods becomes legitimate for this control, but it is immoral to perform the sexual act preventing procreation.

Pius XI ratifies this position by evoking a comment by Saint Augustine to the biblical account of Onan, son of the Patriarch Judah. The eldest son of Judah married Tamar and died without descendants. Tamar then married her brother-in-law, Onan, to beget offspring from the family of her late husband, according to the levirate law. But Onan, by having sex with her, practiced *coitus interuptus*. He wasted semen and did not comply with the law. Therefore, he was punished by God with death (cf. Gen 38:8–10). Augustine warns that: "even with the legitimate woman, the act of marriage is unlawful and dishonest when the conception of offspring is avoided. So did Onan son of Judah, and God killed him." The pope, in turn, reiterates the warning: "Any use of marriage in which, by human malice, the act is stripped of its natural procreative force, infringes the law of God and nature, and those who dare to commit such actions become guilty defendants."[54] His successor, Pius XII, considers this law something perennial: "This prescription is in full force today as yesterday, and it will still be tomorrow and always."[55]

A few years after the council, Paul VI finally ruled on birth control by publishing the encyclical *Humanae Vitae*. He holds the position of the magisterium of the Church and dares not distance himself from it. Conjugal acts are legitimate if they are expected to be infertile, but they must remain open to the transmission of life, excluding direct sterilization and any action that makes procreation impossible.[56] This teaching, however, is not put into practice by the majority of the Catholic faithful and is questioned by a considerable number of theologians. For those who question the encyclical, with the reestablishment by the council of the relational purpose of marriage and sexual intercourse, the judgment on the morality of the sexual act should be drawn up not based on the act, but in the place of the act in its relational context. Some episcopal conferences have even stated that in the event of marital conflicts arising from the application of the encyclical, the faithful must follow their own conscience.

In a brief overview of sex in the Catholic world, at the doctrinal level, it lost the negative connotation and had its relational dimension valued but remains "conjugal" in the exclusive and indissoluble union between a man and a woman, within the reproductive model. As a form of birth control, only sexual abstinence is accepted during the fertile periods. In practice, of course, the reality is quite different.

PATHS AND INSTRUMENTS OF THEOLOGICAL REFLECTION

Christian morality, born from the impulse of faith, has been formed throughout history with elements of the Jewish, Hellenistic (Greco-Roman), and Western worlds. In this long enculturation, three great paradigms can be identified at its roots:

- Ascetic reason, predominant in patristic times, influenced by Stoicism and Platonism. It results in a moral code of virtues (faced with the "vices" of the pagans, in which chastity is configured), sexual restriction (even in married life), and procreation (as a general justification for sexual life).
- Natural reason, predominant in the Middle Ages and the post-Tridentine period. Through Saint Albert the Great and Saint Thomas Aquinas, Aristotelian anthropology is embraced, and sexuality is considered a natural faculty and teleology. Moral codes of sexual behavior are organized around a moderate and virtuous use, which respects the "natural order" and teleological sexuality, that is, its procreative purpose. This paradigm developed at the time of Casuist and post-Tridentine morality, with a general tendency toward rigorism, considering the transgression of the sixth and ninth commandments always a serious matter.
- Personal reason, since the Second Vatican Council. The person is situated as an appropriate reference for

> the understanding and realization of sexual life. The personalist paradigm, under the influence of Kant and modern personalist culture, gives relevance to the values of the "I," the "relationship with the you" and the "we." Sexuality belongs more to the realm of freedom than to the realm of nature; it is considered more in the positive aspect than in a pessimistic anthropological understanding or an ascetic and abstentionist moral.[57]

The personalist paradigm in the area of sexuality was defended by the theologian Joseph Ratzinger (later Pope Benedict XVI) a few years after the council. For him, chastity is not a physiological but a social virtue. It is about humanizing sexuality, not "naturalizing it." Its humanization consists in considering it not as a means of private satisfaction, a kind of numbing within the reach of all, but as an invitation for humans to go outside themselves. The act of sexuality does not acquire an ethical value when it is made "according to nature," but when it occurs according to the responsibility that the human being has before the other, before the human community, and before the human future. To evaluate sexuality, it can be said that it reflects and concretizes the fundamental dilemma of the human person. It can represent the total liberation of self in the other, or also the total alienation and closing in on oneself.

To clarify his proposition, Ratzinger turned to the Old Testament, where there are two groups of norms related to sexuality: moral and cultic. For the first group, only the social aspect was decisive and the physiological was not considered. For the second, only the physiological aspect mattered, but without any moral valence. "The disgrace of ecclesiastical moral theology," he asserts, frequently consisted in having converted the Old Testament's cultic precepts into moral obligations. Therefore, the passage from the old to the new law was nothing more than a misunderstanding.[58]

Well, not everything he taught later as cardinal and as pope goes along this line. But based on these reflections and some of the teachings of Ratzinger's pontificate, one can go further and ask: Are there points of morality that reveal a lack of fruitful dialogue between believers and nonbelievers, between philosophers, jurists, and scientists? Is there still a passive submission to the physical laws of nature, an imposition on the consciousness of law from the outside, or undue naturalization of anthropological positions? Are there responsible behaviors in the field of sexuality that are not properly recognized and valued? Where are the misfortunes of ecclesiastical morality, where the old law has not passed to the new one? The chapters of this book contain many positions and doctrines about which one can reflect on these questions.

There is a classicist worldview of natural law, in which a sexual act has an intrinsic meaning independent of the relational meaning of that act to humans. In this view, there are basic goods desired that give reason to human choices. These seem more generic goods or Platonic ideas, detached from concrete reality, people, and interpersonal relationships. It is an act-centered morality that has absolute norms. A *personalist* view of natural law is interested in the meaning of sexual acts for human relations, before asking biological questions about genitalia or similar. This view emphasizes historical consciousness, the particularity of the basic goods and the person, and the norms that reflect this particularity, constituting a morality centered on the relationship. Augustine argues that all true virtues are instructed by charity, and without charity, there is no true virtue. Aquinas argues that justice not instructed by charity lacks perfection but remains a virtue. There may be tension between virtues. Classicism limits dialectics between virtues, while historical consciousness recognizes that virtues challenge and define each other.[59]

One can agree with most Catholic moral theologians that there are absolute ethical norms and that these norms dispel confusion. However, it is worth adding what the theologian Dietmar Mieth says: the only absolute norm is that "we must do good, not evil," and any other ethical judgment requires a concrete and empirical judgment. Josef Fuchs also agrees. For him, there is no discrepancy between theories and opinions in Catholic moral theology about the only ethical absolute, but the translation of this absolute into the material and concrete plurality of human reality is another matter. The exercise of this translation, in the Catholic moral tradition, is controlled by the reason that seeks to be attentive, intelligent, and responsible in dealing with the sociohistorical reality. It is not possible to be different in front of free people, who live in a world that is simultaneously physical, human, and subject to historicity.[60]

Historicity is somewhat contemplated in the teaching of the *Catechism* on creation. This "has its own goodness and proper perfection, but it did not spring forth complete from the hands of the Creator. The universe was created 'in a state of journeying' (*in statu viae*) toward an ultimate perfection yet to be attained, to which God has destined it" (CCC, 1997, n. 302). Nature, in a classicist view, evokes a homogeneous and harmonious reality from the idea of the cosmos. It is a symbol of immutability. But an unfinished creation makes nature a symbol of uncertainty. One should not let it act blindly. We must lead it, acting responsibly. This may feel like being in front of a broken mirror, which no longer reflects the image one had of oneself, of the creatures, and of the Creator himself. But it is the chance to find other references or worldviews in which contrasting forces interact, and harmony and complexity come together.[61]

There are new paths to follow. It is worth noting the remarkable difference between the teaching of the Catholic Church in the social field and the teaching in the sexual and family fields. In the first, there is clarity of principles and a wide margin reserved for the faithful in concrete mediations and choices. In the second, there is clarity of principles together with a strong attachment to concrete mediations and the choices demanded from the faithful.[62]

In Christ's message the supreme commandment of love is found: "I give you a new commandment, that you love one another. Just as I have loved you, you also should love one another" (John 13:34–35). The Church's social teaching was born from the encounter of the Gospel message and its requirements—summarized in this commandment—with the problems that emanate from life in society. This teaching uses the resources of wisdom and the humanities; it concerns the ethical aspect of social life and considers the technical aspects of problems. Turning to action, such teaching develops amid changing circumstances of history. It has always valid principles, but it involves contingent judgments. Far from constituting a closed system, it remains constantly open to the new questions that always present themselves, and requires the contribution of all charisms, experiences, and skills. In its social doctrine, the Church wants to offer principles of reflection, criteria of judgment, and guidelines for action, so that profound changes are made according to what the situations of misery and injustice require, serving the good of human beings (CDF, 1986a, n. 72). Similarly, in the field of sexuality, what many want today is a system open to new questions, capable of receiving the contribution of all charisms, experiences, and skills, for the fulfillment of the supreme commandment of love.

Related to the doctrine of the Church on sexuality, the following positions of theologians can be identified:

- Some seek to offer a discourse justifying the concrete norms of official morality.
- On the opposite pole, there are those who seek solutions consistent with the Christian faith and in dialogue with the current culture, even if such solutions deviate from the official concrete norm.
- Most Catholic moral theologians are in an intermediate option that seeks to articulate a project of sexual ethics without extrapolating the limits marked by the official doctrine of the Church but seeks to dialogue with the human sciences and with the current personalist culture. It is a balanced option sometimes difficult to understand.[63]

Tradition is a precious value for the Church because it lives on the spiritual and institutional legacy left by Christ and the apostles. This legacy is cultivated, deepened, and developed with the help of the Holy Spirit. The apostolic tradition of the Church is part of the broad mosaic of Judeo-Christian religious and cultural elements, manifest in history. This Tradition (with capital T), as Pope Benedict XVI taught, consists of the transmission of the goods of salvation, which makes the Christian community the permanent updating of its original communion. Thanks to the Spirit, the experience made by the apostolic community in the origins of the Church of the presence of the risen Christ can always be experienced by successive generations because it is transmitted and updated in the faith, worship, and communion of the people of God, a pilgrim in time. The permanent updating of Christ's active presence in his people, carried out by the Spirit, is what characterizes tradition. Through tradition, the water of life that came out of Christ's side and his wholesome blood reach women and men of every age. It is not the transmission of a collection of words or dead things. Tradition is the living river that connects us to the origins, the living river in which the origins are always present.[64]

To this teaching of Pope Benedict, it is necessary to add the warning made by himself many years before:

> Not everything that exists in the Church must for that reason be also a legitimate tradition; in other words, not every tradition that arises in the Church is a true celebration and keeping present of the mystery of Christ. There is a distorting, as well as a legitimate, tradition....Consequently tradition must not be considered only affirmatively but also critically.[65]

The active presence of Christ in the life of his people involves the humanization of sexuality, as an invitation to the human being to come out of themself. The exercise of sexuality does not acquire ethical value when it is done according to a supposed homogeneous, harmonious, and immutable nature, but when it occurs according to the responsibility that the human being has before the other, the community, and the future of humanity. May theology be duly critical and constructive concerning tradition.

2

THE EMERGENCE OF GENDER AND SEXUAL-ORIENTATION ISSUES

One of the most notable features of the world today is the visibility of the LGBTQ+ population, consisting of lesbians, gays bisexuals, transvestites, and transsexuals. They are gender-related identities and sexual orientations. Traditionally, gender is defined as what identifies and differentiates men and women. It is synonymous with sexual organs and to what is proper to males as well as to females. However, from the perspective of social sciences and psychology, gender is understood as what differentiates people socially, considering historical-cultural patterns attributed to men and women. In recent decades, gender studies have also been related to sexual orientation. Frequently, they serve as a basis for strong sociopolitical activism and the implementation of public policies. Some research and reflections show the role of culture and social structures in the configuration and relationship between genders, question the subalternity from one gender to another, and contemplate the reality of the LGBTQ+ population.

To clarify some terms, transvestites are people who experience female roles but do not recognize themselves as men or as women. The term is always used in the feminine in Portuguese: as *travestis*. Transsexuals, in turn, are people who do not identify with the sex assigned to them at birth, but with the other sex. There may be transgender men, who claim social and legal recognition as men, and transsexual women, who claim social and legal recognition as women. Both transvestites and transsexuals are transgender (or simply "trans"), that is, people who do not identify with the sex assigned to them at birth. The opposite of transgender is cisgender, which refers to the person identified with the sex assigned at birth.[1]

An international convention established principles for the enforcement of human rights legislation regarding sexual orientation and gender identity. They are the Yogyakarta Principles whose definitions were widely accepted even in Brazilian legislation:

I. Sexual orientation refers "to each person's capacity for profound emotional, affectional and sexual attraction to, and intimate and sexual relations with, individuals of a different gender or the same gender or more than one gender."
II. Gender identity refers "to each person's deeply felt internal and individual experience of gender, which may or may not correspond with the sex assigned at birth, including the personal sense of the body (which may involve, if freely chosen, modification of bodily appearance or function by medical, surgical or other means) and other expressions of gender, including dress, speech, and mannerisms."[2]

With this classification, lesbian, gay, homosexual, bisexual, or heterosexual are concepts that refer to *sexual orientation*. In turn, transvestites, transsexuals, transgender, and cisgender refer to *gender identity*. The term *sexual diversity*, although somewhat imprecise, is used today for issues related to the LGBTQ+ population. Some governments have coordination offices on sexual-diversity issues. A set of federal law proposals prepared by the Brazilian Bar Association is called the Statute of Sexual and Gender Diversity.[3]

In the past, to defend themselves from intolerance and hostility, many LGBTQ+ people lived anonymously or on the margins of society. Some formed ghettos, which were very private living spaces where they felt safe. Several gays and lesbians hid in traditional marriages, constituted by the heterosexual union, not to manifest their condition. Today, however, they all make big parades, are present in films, television, Olympics, companies, schools, and other institutions, and seek recognition, demand respect, and claim the same rights and duties as other citizens. This population is everywhere. Those who are not part of it either have close or distant relatives who are part of it, publicly or privately, as well as neighbors or coworkers.

Sexualities and diverse genders have a complex history in the West and their interaction with the Judeo-Christian tradition, and since the recent past have been beneficiaries of the development and expansion of modernity.

A HISTORICAL ITINERARY

Classical antiquity did not present homosexuality in opposition to heterosexuality, but a bisexuality whose manifestations were commanded by chance encounters and not by biological determinisms. The word and concept of homosexuality did not exist, but rather the sexual desire and sexual practice of same-sex people. Love and intimacy among men are exalted by Plato, but also by the Latin authors. Regarding this issue, there is nothing to distinguish between Greek and Latin authors. The so-called Greek love could be called Roman love with the same legitimacy. Catullus boasts of his feats. Cicero sang the kisses he took from the lips of his slave and secretary. According to the tastes of each one, women, boys, or both were chosen. Virgil liked exclusively boys, and the emperor Claudius liked women. Horace repeats that he loves both sexes. The poets freely sang the beauties of the young favorite of the emperor Domitian. It is known that Antinous, a young favorite of Emperor Hadrian, received an official cult after his early death.

Catullus's poetry is full of insults whereby the poet threatens to penetrate his enemies sexually to characterize the triumph over them. In the Mediterranean environment, they were common folk conquests: the important thing is to penetrate, no matter the sex of the other person. To be active was to be manly, the partner, whatever the sex, was called passive. The fundamental question was whether to have pleasure in a manly way or to give pleasure in a servile way. Married women, virgins, and teenagers free by birth should be respected. The supposed legal repression of homosexuality was aimed at preventing a citizen from being penetrated as a slave. A colossal contempt fell upon the adult and free man who allowed himself to be passive, or as they said, *impudicus*. In Greece, the ephebi, or young people, who were not yet citizens, could be passive without dishonor, as well as the slaves in Rome, even if they were children. In that slave society, a virtue was made of necessity with the proverb: "There is no shame in doing what the master commands."

In general, Roman society did not ask whether men practiced sex with other men, but paid enormous attention to details of the garments, pronunciation, gestures, and manner of walking. Those who manifested any lack of virility were strongly despised, regardless of their sexual preferences. The state even banned opera shows because they were less virile, unlike gladiator shows. There was a rejection of female homoerotism, especially the active mistress, because a woman taken as a man is the world inside out. There was equal horror for the women who "ride" the men, according to Seneca.[4]

Outside of the Western tradition, there are in history many examples of what we now call sexual and gender diversity, from the far east to the far west. In Islamic Sufi literature, homoeroticism was an important metaphorical expression of the spiritual relationship between God and humans. Much of the Persian poetry and fiction that present examples of moral love employs gay relations. Among the ancient Chinese, the most popular literary expression for love between men was "passion of the cut sleeve." It was an allusion to the selfless devotion of the last emperor of the Han dynasty, Ai Ti. Upon being called to an audience, he cut the sleeve of his shirt so as not to wake up his lover Tung Hsien, who slept on it.[5]

In many American and Canadian indigenous tribes, some people played many mixed-gender roles, including dressing up and performing male and female works. This has been documented in over 130 tribes. In sixteenth-century Brazil, a colonizer witnessed the disinhibition of Tupinambás in the practice of homoerotism, which he calls nefarious sin, that is, something so perverse that it should not even be named. The Tupinambás were "very fond of nefarious sin, among which they do not have as an affront; and the one who serves as a male, is brave, and tells this bestiality for prowess; and in their villages for the backlands, there are some who have a public tent to those who want them as public women."[6]

In Brazilian religions of African origins, such as Umbanda and Candomblé, there is a remarkable acceptance of homosexual people, already noted by the American anthropologist Ruth Landes in the

1940s, at a time of visible social opposition to homosexuality. In the Black community of Bahia, she says, unusual circumstances spur some passive homosexuals to forge a new and respectable status for themselves. Entering Candomblé in an influential way, as *pais de santo* (saint fathers), they have a voice in all vital activities and are kept and highly esteemed by those "normal" men for whom they were once the target of mockery and derision.[7]

In the Judeo-Christian tradition, since its inception, homoerotism has been condemned. To understand this condemnation, one must bear in mind the historicity of the revelation transmitted in Sacred Scripture, as taught by Pope Pius XII and the Second Vatican Council in the previous chapter. One must seek the meaning that the sacred authors in certain circumstances, according to the conditions of their time and their culture, intended to express using the literary genres that were then in use. This sense is linked to the broader context of the ancient times of the East so the current interpreter must use history, archaeology, ethnology, and other sciences that contribute to their proper understanding.

According to ancient Jewish cosmology expressed in the Bible, the universe was created in six days. The earth appeared before the sun and the stars and is immovable. The celestial vault, called "firmament," is a solid plate on which the stars are hung so that they do not fall. There are no loose stars in the sky. The firmament is supported by columns and divides the waters above it from the waters below. The rain is not the result of the condensation of the water vapor, but of the floodgates of the firmament that open, causing the upper dammed waters to fall. This is how the universal flood occurred in Noah's time. There is also anthropology in which man came straight from the dust of the earth, and a woman came from the rib of man.

It was believed that man and woman were created for each other, to unite and procreate. A universal heterosexuality is presupposed, expressed in the imperative "Be fruitful and multiply" (Gen 1:28). This was written at the time of the Jewish exile in Babylon. For the people expelled from their land and subjected to a foreign power, being fertile was fundamental to the survival of the nation, culture, and religion. There was no denial of the divine plan that humanity should spread across the earth, but the need for the survival of the Jewish people at that time was urgent.

The man's semen supposedly contained the entire human being and was to be placed in the womb of the woman just as the seed is deposited in the earth. It should never be wasted, as the account of Onan shows. He married Tamar, the widow of his brother Er, who died without children. According to the law (cf. Deut 25:5–10), Onan was to raise a posterity to his brother, and the first male son was to bear the name of this deceased brother, Er. But Onan practiced interrupted coitus, ejaculating out of his wife's vagina, and preventing her from conceiving. Therefore, he was struck down by God, as punishment for this transgression (cf. Gen 38:1–10).

It is in this context that sexual intercourse between two men was considered an abomination. Israel was to distinguish itself from other nations in various ways, through its faith, its worship, its law, and its customs, according to the holiness code of the Book of Leviticus. This includes the prohibition of homoeroticism, considered an abomination (cf. Lev 18:22). It is also strictly forbidden to work on the Sabbath day, to eat pork or seafood, to trim hair and beard, to touch a menstruated woman for seven days, to wear clothes woven with two species of yarn, to plant different species of seed in the same field, and mate animals of distinct species. When Christianity, born in Israel, expanded among non-Jewish peoples, the holiness of Leviticus did not become the norm for these peoples, but the prohibition of homoerotism did.

Adding weight to this prohibition was the story of Sodom and Gomorrah, whose sin cried out to heaven and resulted in destructive divine punishment (Gen 19). This sin was to refuse hospitality to those who visited the patriarch Lot, to the point of trying to sexually rape him. Sexual violence was often a form of humiliation imposed by winning armies on the vanquished. Initially, the crime of Sodom was that it "had pride, excess of food, and prosperous ease, but did not aid the poor and needy." Through the prophet, the Lord says, "They were haughty, and did abominable things before me" (Ezek 16:49–50). Several centuries later, such a sin was identified with homoerotism, but in origin, it has nothing to do with love between people of the same sex, or even with freely consented sexual relations between same-sex adults.

There is a similar account of Sodom's sin in the book of Judges (cf. Judg 19 and 20). A Levite and his concubine stayed in the city of Gibeah of the Benjamin tribe. The townspeople harassed the visitors and raped the Levite's concubine to death. The Lord raised the Israelites against that city, and it was destroyed. From this account, one should not condemn heterosexuality. What is condemned—both in

Sodom and in Gibeah—is the lack of hospitality and violent hostility toward outsiders.

In the allusions to Sodom and Gomorrah in the Gospels (cf. Matt 10:15; 11:23–24; Luke 17:28–29), there is no mention of homosexual themes. But in the New Testament, two texts refer to these cities with a certain homosexual connotation. The Epistle of Jude refers to the carnal relationship between men and almost divine beings: "sexual immorality and pursued unnatural lust" (vv. 7–8). The text of 2 Peter reproves the "licentiousness of the lawless," who are carried away by their "flesh in depraved lust" (2 Pet 2:6–10). How then did the homosexual interpretation come about? It appears to have been through intertestamental writings, such as the Testament of Benjamin 9, and the II Secrets of Enoch 10:4 and 34:1–2. To these Apocrypha are added the writings of Philo of Alexandria and Josephus. In contact with the Hellenistic world, such Jewish writings interpreted Sodom's account as a clear reference to homosexual behavior. The two New Testament texts (Jude 7–8; 2 Pet 2:6–8) are linked to this interpretation.[8]

In the New Testament, the most important text on homoeroticism is found in the Letter of Saint Paul to the Romans. The apostle says that whoever loves his neighbor has fulfilled the law because the commandments are limited to loving his neighbor as himself (cf. Rom 13:8–10). This is the spirit of the commandments and the criterion of their interpretation. But in refuting polytheism, Paul associates it with homoerotism (cf. Rom 1:18–32). The pagans did not worship the one God, but the creatures. They still allowed this sexual practice seen as an abomination by the Jews. This behavior is considered divine punishment because of a wrong religious practice: "For this reason God gave them up to degrading passions" (Rom 1:26). Other Pauline writings have the same position, where possible references to homoeroticism are linked to idolatry and irreligion (1 Cor 6:9–11; 1 Tim 1:8–11).

In the Judeo-Christian context of antiquity, this argument was understandable. There was no concept of sexual orientation, an inclination deeply rooted in the person, with relative stability, attracting them to the opposite sex or the same sex. This orientation has nothing to do with belief in one or several gods, or any religious practice. But in antiquity, the Church inherited the Jewish anthropological view of universal heterosexuality with its interdictions and carried it for centuries. Today, however, one cannot use Paul's argument, for it would be like telling a heterosexual person that if they adhere to a pagan religion, they will become homosexual. This is unfounded. It's a superstition.

The Christian religion expanded in the Roman Empire and became hegemonic, becoming a state religion in late antiquity. Thus, Christianity was formed, a political-religious fusion with a Christian basis that was adopted by kingdoms and empires, medieval and modern, in much of the West and a part of the East. In Christianity, homoerotism was classified as sodomy, and it was criminalized for many centuries in several places. There are examples of strong execration, as in the First Constitutions of the Archbishopric of Bahia, 1707. This legal-pastoral document of colonial Brazil states that sodomy is a horrendous crime: it provokes the wrath of God to the point of causing storms, earthquakes, plagues, and famines that destroy entire cities. It is something unworthy of being named, a "nefarious sin" of which one should not speak, let alone commit.[9] Civil and ecclesiastical courts, such as the Inquisition, tried those accused of this crime. The guilty were handed over to the civil power to be punished, even with death.

Such denouncement of sodomy is also found in civil laws, such as the Philippine Ordinations, a code of 1603 in force throughout the Iberian Peninsula and in the Portuguese and Spanish colonies:

> Let every person, of any quality whatsoever, that sin of sodomy, per any way, commit, be burned and made by fire to dust; lest there be a memory of his body and grave; and all his possessions be confiscated for the Crown of our kingdom, though he has descendants; by the same case his sons and grandsons will be disabled and infamous, as well as those of those who commit the crime of lese-majesty.
>
> 1. And this Law we also want to be understood for women, that among them, commit sin against the nature and the way we have said in men.[10]

All this horror has an explanation. There was in the past, from antiquity to the eighteenth century, a wide involvement of the supernatural. It was believed that storms, earthquakes, pests, and agricultural plagues, condemning entire populations to starvation, were direct interventions of God in the world as punishment for the sins of humanity. Many biblical accounts corroborate this involvement: the flood in Noah's time; the plagues in Egypt against Pharaoh; the storm at sea in the episode in which the prophet Jonah was swallowed by a fish; the punishment chosen by King David among the options offered by God through the prophet: famine, pestilence, and defeat by enemies (cf. 2 Sam 24:1–24); and, of course, the destruction of Sodom and Gomorrah.

The practice of homoerotism, however discreet, was not just a matter of the private life of the people directly involved. At the end of the fifteenth century, the Kingdom of Venice suffered a military defeat against the Turks, who took the fortress of Modon in Greece. Consequently, the Venetian laws against blasphemy and sodomy hardened to counter the supposed causes of defeat. Sodomy was something that threatened all society, such as the crime of *lèse-majesté*—an offense or defamation committed against the king, against any member of the royal family, or the sovereign power of a state. Therefore, the punishment for both crimes was equally severe.

Despite the widespread condemnation of homoerotism by Christianity, signs of possible tolerance should be noted. John Boswell thoroughly examined signs of affection among saints of the same sex, as well as in monastic life in antiquity and the early Middle Ages. He gives importance to the pairs of saints, such as Perpetua and Felicity, Polyeuctus and Nearchus, Sergius and Bacchus; and to the exchange of love poetry, as between Ausonius and Saint Paulinus of Nola. Boswell's hermeneutic perspective points to an understanding or, at least, to a not excessive condemnation of homosexuality (1995). But there is a lack of research to discern with sufficient objectivity these signs of affection.

Boswell purports to have discovered in the medieval period signs of tolerance in a detailed analysis of practices of love between equals, made by clerics and monks, and tolerated by the Church. Among these practices stands out the "wedding of similarity," which was a form of union, like a brotherhood or fraternity, celebrated in a ceremony with commitments similar to marriage between a man and a woman. For the author, the contemporary homosexual community should seek past references not so much in Socrates's Greece, but in the medieval twelfth century, when clerics wrote love poems to their friends and tolerated weddings among equals. This situation changed radically in the fourteenth century, when Western Europe acquired a furious obsession with homosexuality, considered the most horrible of sins.[11]

The historical question is not only whether same-sex relationships have been tolerated, which seems evident, but whether they have been recognized in society with a similar status to marriage. The author argues that yes, at least in some European regions of Greek influence. The sources used by Boswell in favor of his thesis include interesting liturgical texts and fraternity documents. But they are very heterogeneous texts with different values of proof. As he acknowledges, there are serious problems with interpretation and philology, and they are limited to certain regions. This means that the conclusions he reaches should be evaluated very carefully. Some researchers claim that there is no basis for considering weddings of similarity the same as same-sex unions in pre-modern Europe.[12]

MODERNITY AND CHANGE

The urban Middle Ages began a long-lasting historical process that triggered a series of sociopolitical, economic, and cultural changes that shaped the contemporary world. This process that brings us to this day and is known as modernity. Its formation accelerated in the sixteenth and seventeenth centuries and was consolidated specifically in the eighteenth and nineteenth centuries. This historical and cultural trajectory involves multiple actors and factors of diverse nature. Modernity was driven and gradually defined in the Scientific and Industrial Revolutions, through the Renaissance, the Protestant Reformation, the Enlightenment, and the contrasting tendencies and liberal and revolutionary movements. Modernity asserted itself in the U.S.-American, French, and Soviet Revolutions, and in the watershed that was established with the philosophy of Descartes about scholastics, and unfolded under the name of modern philosophy, which encompasses widely diverse and even contradictory thought trends.

Modernity was shaped in the natural and social sciences, as well as in the ideologies and economic processes that began with the monetary and commercial revolutions at the end of the Middle Ages. Modernity is the process that generated the autonomy of the secular state, bureaucratization, the separation between public and private, the creation of nation-states and, later, the capitalist or socialist socioeconomic and political systems, in various versions and nuances, in the various historical achievements of the nineteenth and twentieth centuries. Modernity was affirmed and spread in European colonial expansion and neocolonial pressure of an economic and political nature. This complex process involved the arts, literature, the education system, research, and religion. Modernity is the result of a slow and long-lasting movement that has profoundly transformed peoples' daily lives.

It simultaneously generated and received processes of sociocultural change, provoking subtle exchanges or even violent shocks of senses, values, techniques, and new ways of acting, communicating, and proceeding. Modernity should not be distinguished from economic, political, and cultural modernity, for it draws attention to different aspects of this macrostructure.[13]

Some fundamental elements or assumptions of the internal structure of modernity can be indicated as:

- The centrality of the individual, subject of rights, decisions, and actions. The individual has legitimacy without necessary reference to the group or dependence on it. There is an emphasis on the formation of individual consciousness and personal responsibility.
- Secularization, which is the affirmation of intramundane or secular reality, and its autonomy. Modern culture inaugurates a new way of thinking and standing before the world, which gradually separates itself from religion, affirming the autonomy of human and earthly realities in the face of any revelation. There is an emancipation of the various spheres of human knowledge and action concerning religion, as well as the mentality and structures fostered by it. Secularization focused on politics, with the separation of church and state that put an end to Christendom, as well as philosophy, law, science, economy, society, and culture.
- The plurality of autonomous knowledge, resulting from the fragmentation of a comprehensive worldview that unified and ranked knowledge. Each field of knowledge begins to develop with its epistemology and methodology, producing a relatively autonomous discourse that does not necessarily articulate with others, as if they were all constellations of a starry sky. The result of this is pluralism. In modernity, it is not primarily a manifestation of tolerance, but a structural consequence of this autonomy of diverse knowledge in the process of interaction.

- The mutual feedback between science and technology contributes to the constant transformations that characterize modernity. Contemporary technologies form systems that affect individual and collective consciousness, with great impact on everyday life, and quietly influence the whole of culture and society.
- An open and dynamic conception of history, with the protagonism of human reason and will, in contrast to the cyclical or static vision of history, which marks many nonmodern cultures. In these, the human being is submissive to history and, in a way, endures history, defenseless and unable to transform it or give it a new direction. Open and dynamic history comes from the Judeo-Christian tradition, which sees the world as creation, the human being endowed with autonomy and free will as a continuer of the Creator's work, and historical time as an interval between creation and eschatological fullness, that is, ultimate and definitive. The modern vision clashes with the Christian vision when historical time is understood in a purely intramundane and immanent way.

The advent of the Enlightenment and autonomous reason brought with it the conviction that sexual practice, exercised without violence or public indecency, should not fall under the rule of law. With the Napoleonic Code in France in 1804, the decriminalization of sodomy in the West began. This was only possible thanks to a worldview in which natural disasters, as well as other evils that afflict society, come to have an immanent explanation other than divine punishment for certain human conducts. However, sodomy was still criminalized in other Western countries. In England, this crime led to the arrest of writer Oscar Wilde in 1895. Computer science pioneer Alan Turing was prosecuted in 1952. In order not to be arrested, he had to undergo hormonal treatment and chemical castration. In Germany, sodomy only began to be decriminalized in the 1970s. The apex of the terror against "homosexuals" was during Nazism when thousands of them were imprisoned in concentration camps, where they received a uniform with a pink triangle and where most of them died.

It should be noted that the term homosexuality, referring to the attraction between people of the same sex, appears in the second half of the nineteenth century. This term appears publicly in two anonymous pamphlets published in Leipzig in 1869, attributed to the Austro-Hungarian writer Karl-Maria Benkert, who later adopted the name Kertbeny. In the pamphlets, the Prussian law on sodomy is accused of violating the rights of men proclaimed in the French Revolution, for in libertarian tradition mutually consenting sexual acts of private life should not fall under criminal law. Prussian law is also accused of favoring blackmail and extortion of money made to homosexuals, which often led them to suicide. That is what happened to a friend of Benkert's youth.

This author argues that homosexuality is innate and immutable, which contradicted the dominant view that men practiced sodomy only because they had a bad character. These men were not effeminate by nature, as the example of many heroes in history demonstrates. The term homosexual is part of its classificatory system of sexual types to replace the pejorative "pederast" (etymologically: a man who has an erotic relationship with a boy), then in vogue in Germany and France. Benkert also designated men who are sexually attracted to women as heterosexual. He was the first writer to have the courage to publish these arguments, a topic so familiar today.[14]

Gradually, however, through the global process of secularization within intellectual circles, the link of sodomy to crime and sin was exchanged for the link of homosexuality to disease and pathology, which does not deserve punishment and penance, but psychiatric treatment or medical cure. The term ended up a prisoner to the interpretative sphere of perversion, fetish, or sexual neurosis, constituting a separate chapter in the manuals of psychopathology, alongside other mental illnesses.

Stigmatization as a pathology had negative repercussions among the public and confirmed the social taboo. The isolation of sexual acts was broken, as they came to be seen in the overall picture of the homosexual person and their basic inclinations. Through the novelty of terminology, several definitions and explanatory theories emerged in psychiatry and psychoanalysis that keep the homosexual within the framework of abnormality, in a fine mixture of minority, anomaly, and condemnation. Apparently, not even Freud escaped that. He wrote to a North American mother that homosexuality is not addiction, degeneration, or disease, as public opinion thought, but a variable of sexual function. This variable is a consequence of premature stagnation in the evolution of libido, which needs treatment. To remove homosexuality from this shadow and free it from the accent on sexual activity, other terms were released, such as homophilia, homoerotism, and homotropy, but had little infiltration in common language.[15]

Currently, the term "gay" is widely used, which comes from English and means primarily cheerful and jovial, thus having a positive connotation. This term probably originates from the Provençal *gai*, used in the late Middle Ages to refer to courtly love and its literature. This word remains in Catalan—a language that is related to Provençal—to designate the art of poetry, a lover, and an openly homosexual person. In the early twentieth century, the term "gay" was common in the English homosexual subculture as a form of code. Decades later, it became popular in the United States through cinema,[16] becoming a program of life and a banner for the emancipatory struggle of homosexuals.

In the second half of the nineteenth century and throughout the twentieth century, it can be said that medicine tried or proposed everything for the cure of homosexuals. Confinement, electric shock, heavy medication, psychological or psychiatric treatment, individual, group, and family psychoanalysis, straitjacket, and testicular transplantation, were techniques of intervention in the body and mind of men who preferred to relate affectively and sexually to other men.

In 1972, for example, there was a symposium of debates on "homosexualism" in Belo Horizonte, Brazil. The main exhibitor of the event was a psychiatrist and professor at the Federal University of Minas Gerais. He advised psychoanalytical and electroshock treatment, but he recognized that psychoanalytic treatment, even prolonged, is almost always doomed to failure. This psychiatrist preferred the treatment he called "aversive": he projected on a screen a picture of a woman and caused the patient to receive pleasant electric waves in the brain; if the photo was of a man, he received an electric shock.[17]

The fight for LGBTQ+ rights will be linked to human rights—the face of modernity linked to the centrality of the individual. Benkert's pamphlet in Germany, referring to the human rights proclaimed in the French Revolution, is an example of this link. The first human rights declarations dealt with freedom and equality, but sexual diversity was not in mind. This approach is due to social and mental changes that bring new perspectives and possibilities.

In the United States, the Declaration of Independence states "that all men are created equal, that they are endowed by their Creator with certain unalienable Rights, that among these are Life, Liberty and the pursuit of Happiness" (Declaration of Independence, July 4, 1776). In the years of the French Revolution, it was proclaimed that "men are born and remain free and equal in rights. Social distinctions may be based only on considerations of the common good. The aim of every political association is the preservation of the natural and imprescriptible rights of Man. These rights are Liberty, Property, Safety and Resistance to Oppression" (Declaration of Human and Civil Rights of 26 August 1789). These rights have a growing adherence to the laws of several nations. After World War II, the newly constituted United Nations (U.N.) proclaimed the Universal Declaration of Human Rights (1948), signed by more than a hundred countries, showing a broad international consensus on values and ideals to be achieved. All of it is based on the recognition of the inherent dignity of all members of the human family and the recognition of their equal and inalienable rights. These rights are considered the foundation of freedom, justice, and peace in the world.

According to Norberto Bobbio, human rights are historical and not immutable and universal. They are born at the beginning of the modern era, together with the conception of society based on the individual's centrality. Moving from the priority of the duties of the subjects to the priority of the rights of the citizen emerged a different way of seeing the political relationship where the angle of the sovereign no longer predominates, but the citizen. The organicist vision of society gives way to the emergence of the individual. Human rights are born amid struggles to defend new freedoms against old powers. They are born gradually, not all at once, and not once and for all. Religious freedom is an effect of religious wars; civil liberties are an effect of the struggle of parliaments against absolute sovereigns; political freedom and social laws are an effect of the emergence of wageworkers and peasant movements.

Changes in society create new needs and new demands. These arise due to changing social conditions and when technical development makes way to allow for these new needs and demands. Human rights are born when they can or should be, and eventually become one of the main indicators of historical progress. The Universal Declaration of Human Rights represents humanity's historical awareness of its fundamental values in the mid-twentieth century.[18]

THE RECENT PANORAMA: DATA, ACHIEVEMENTS, AND PROBLEMS

In the recent past, there have been other demands that constitute new developments in human rights: equality between men and women, racial equality and the end of segregation, socio-environmental rights, repudiation of discrimination against LGBTQ+ people, and recognition of their unions. The depathologization of homosexuality began. The American Psychiatric Association removed homosexuality from its list of diseases in 1973. The Federal Council of Medicine in Brazil also did so in 1985. The World Health Organization made this same decision in an assembly held on May 17, 1990. The decision came into force a few years later, and May 17 became for social movements the World Day to Combat Homophobia. Since 1991, Amnesty International has considered discrimination or any act of violence against homosexuals as a violation of human rights. In 1999, the Federal Council of Psychology in Brazil declared that homosexuality is not a disease, disorder, or perversion, and prohibited psychologists from collaborating in services that propose their treatment and cure. In 2018, the same council depathologized transvestite and transsexual identities.

Homosexuality and transgenderism are not an option. In the case of a homosexual or heterosexual person, it is about sexual orientation; and gender identity, in the case of a cisgender or transgender person, that is, one who respectively identifies or not with the sex assigned to them at birth. It is not voluntarily reversible. Statistics on the homosexual population vary. According to the World Health Organization, 10 percent of the world's total population is homo- or bisexual. Others say surely 4 percent are homosexuals.

This classification needs to be nuanced with other data. In an extensive report published in the 1940s, biologist Alfred Kinsey stated that the population cannot be divided into two distinct groups, homosexual and heterosexual. The real world is a *continuum*, where there is a gradual sequence. Both he and Freud believed that humans are born with erotic responsiveness to both sexes and that social factors inclined most to prefer one or the other. On a scale of one to five, men would be successively: (1) predominantly heterosexual and only incidentally homosexual, (2) predominantly heterosexual and more than incidentally homosexual, (3) equivalently homosexual and heterosexual, items (4) and (5) are the inverse of (1) and (2). If this approach is correct, gays are sufficiently on the homosexual end of the Kinsey scale to consider themselves predominantly homosexual.[19]

There is also an important biopsychic component in homosexuality and transgenderism. According to some neuroscientists, it is the brain and not the genitalia or sex hormones that define sexual attraction and gender identity. In sexual attraction, there are odors linked to masculinity and femininity, and pheromones that, when inhaled, are identified by the brain and influence perception and behavior. In the animal world, these odors are fundamental in the approximation between the sexes and in mating. Specialized CT scans reveal that the brain of homosexual women responds to pheromones differently from the brain of heterosexual women, and like that of heterosexual men. That is, both gay women and straight men are attracted to women. Similar experiments with homosexual men came to opposite and symmetrical results. The brains of these men respond to pheromones differently from the brains of heterosexual men, and similarly to heterosexual women. That is, homosexual men and heterosexual women are attracted to men.[20] In the case of transgender people, the brain, and the perception of oneself do not correspond to the genitalia and the rest of the body. The person feels they are a man in a woman's body; or a woman or transvestite in a man's body.

This biopsychic component also manifests itself in the animal world. Canadian biologist Bruce Bagemihl, author of the book *Biological Exuberance: Animal Homosexuality and Natural Diversity* (1998), cataloged more than three hundred vertebrate species in which genital contact between individuals of the same sex regularly occurs. In some of these species, between 1 and 10 percent of the pairs are of the same sex. In other cases, as in bonobo monkeys, homosexual mating occurs with the same frequency as heterosexual mating. In some species, this only occurs with males; in others, only with females; and in others, with individuals of both sexes. Regarding the length of the bond, there is no rule. There are cases of homosexual couples in which the bonds last for years. There are species in which these unions have a short duration. The widespread occurrence of same-sex vertebrate relationships raises the possibility that even though there is a genetic basis for this behavior, this base has a comprehensive adaptive significance. It will not be an aberrant condition in which only some species are casually trapped.[21]

In addition to the research, the gay movement acquired remarkable visibility in the social field in 1969, when, in front of the Stonewall Inn, a gay bar in New York, a sequence of protests against police raids and humiliations imposed on gays and transgender people took place. These massive and public protests against the oppression they suffered had great repercussions in the media. A year later, in memory of these events, the gay parade that gradually spread throughout the world was created. The gay movement emerged in Brazil during the military dictatorship. Its main icon is the alternative monthly newspaper *Lampião da Esquina*, which began circulating in 1978, taking advantage of the slowdown of censorship. A few years later came the Gay Group of Bahia, which for decades has done remarkable work documenting the homophobic and transphobic crimes committed in Brazil. Homosexuality is still criminalized in more than seventy countries, many of which have a predominantly Muslim population. In some of these countries, there is the death penalty and public executions.

The nomenclature of the gay movement has varied in recent decades. In Brazil, for example, there has been the acronym MHB (Brazilian Homosexual Movement). The Ministry of Health uses the acronym MSM (Men who have Sex with Men) for public policies to prevent sexually transmitted diseases. You can also find the acronym GLS (Gay, Lesbian, and Sympathizers). This last word is a translation of the English expression "gay friendly." The term LGBT was widely recognized in 2008, with a national conference for this population promoted by the federal government.

The visibility of sexual and gender diversity also manifests the problems that afflict the LGBTQ+ population. In many countries, there is a strong aversion to homosexuals—*homophobia*—and transvestites and transsexuals—*transphobia*. This aversion produces various forms of physical, verbal, and symbolic violence against these people. Some fathers say: "I prefer a dead son to a gay son"; and some mothers say: "I prefer a prostitute daughter to a dyke daughter." It is not uncommon for gays and lesbians to be expelled from their homes by their parents. Among the most offensive words that exist in Portuguese are the reference to the homosexual condition (*veado*!) and the reference to anal intercourse (*vai tomar no cu*! that literally translates to "take it in the asshole"), which is common in male homoerotism. Clearly, it is cursing.

Often, when people say, "so-and-so is not a man," you mean he's gay; or "so-and-so is not a woman," she is a lesbian. In other words, being a man or being a woman supposedly excludes the homosexual person. This person is seen as castrated and relegated to subhumanity. The social imaginary of gender is still linked to the patriarchal model, in which the man is expected to be virile, provider, heterosexual, and father; and the woman to be female, domestic, also heterosexual, and mother. Homophobia is deeply rooted in culture. In Brazil, murders are frequent, especially of transvestites. There is also the suicide of many teenagers and even adults, who discover that they are gay or lesbian. They come to this extreme attitude by sensing the hostile rejection of their own family and society. Such hostility generates innumerable forms of discrimination and, even if it does not lead to death, often brings deep sadness or depression.

Father Julio Lancellotti works in the city of São Paulo with the homeless. He recounts the dramatic situation that he encounters:

> In the pastoral mission, I have talked with several LGBTs who are on the streets of the city, some sick, wounded, and abandoned. Many report stories of violence, abuse, harassment, torture, and cruelty. Some tell how they were expelled from churches and Christian communities, and rejected by families in the name of morals. I witnessed tears, wounds, blood, and hunger. Impossible not to recognize in them the presence of the Crucified Lord![22]

In addition to brutal forms of violence and exclusion, there are complaints of subtle forms of subordination and oppression. One of them is the hiding or cover-up of the oppression suffered by a minority against the dominant current that maintains the hegemonic values of a social group. This occurs when an assimilation behavior becomes practically mandatory in a given context, such as the impossibility of gays and lesbians manifesting who they are, or that they cannot come together and/or express affection in public. Even when they find themselves in a situation where others around them know their reality, some kind of concealment is imposed as necessary or desirable. In a way, there is submission to an implicit motto: the outsiders are included, but only if they behave like those inside, practicing a cover-up.[23] There is also the "minority stress," the physical-psychological overload to which an individual is subject when belonging to a minority.[24] This happens with ethnic-racial minorities in racist environments, with women in sexist places, and with homosexuals and transgenders in homophobic and transphobic places. The adverse or hostile environment imposes an overload on them to live, transit, or work with the same performance as the others.

Despite all the adversities, in recent decades there have been important achievements in LGBTQ+ rights. In Brazil, judicial decisions guaranteed widowed spouses of homosexual unions inheritance, pension, and custody of children; the decisions also made possible the adoption of children by these unions, considered homosexual unions as marriage and family with the same rights and obligations as heterosexual unions, and allowed transvestites and transsexuals to change their documents by placing a name that matches their gender identity. Discrimination based on sexual orientation or gender identity has become a crime equated to racism. A new branch of law was created: homoaffective law. Public companies, private companies, and state agencies that grant benefits to their employees and their families also include LGBTQ+, their spouses, and other family members. Some of these institutions promote with remarkable commitment to internal policies for the inclusion of sexual and gender diversity. However, often their homosexual employees do not reveal their sexual orientation and do not enjoy these policies. There is a strong fear of being embarrassed in the workplace by close colleagues. Hiding often wins.

At the government level, there are public policies to combat homophobia and the professionalization of transvestites and transsexuals. The Unified Health System (SUS) performs transsexualizing processes, which enable the transgender person to acquire physical characteristics of the gender with which they identify in their body. These processes may or may not include hormonal treatment, varied surgical procedures such as mastectomy (breast removal) for transsexual men, and genital/sexual reassignment or transgenitalization surgery. This surgery changes the person's genital organ to create a neovagina or neophallus. It is not correct to talk about sex change, because this supposedly is already in the person—in the perception and identification of oneself.[25]

THE EMERGENCE OF NEW ISSUES

The feminist movement brought radical reflections and questions about sexual difference and their social roles. This had an impact on LGBTQ+ thinking and activism. In 1949, Simone de Beauvoir published the book *The Second Sex* with a bombastic phrase: "One is not born a woman, one becomes a woman." This phrase caused a great scandal, and in 1956, the work was included in the Index of Forbidden Books of the Catholic Church. For Beauvoir, being a woman is not a natural fact, it is not explained by biology or even by psychoanalysis. It is a cultural event, the result of the action of processes of symbolic construction that are at the origin of human history. Women who have now acquired the rights of formal equality are faced with the great task of discovering who they are. The feminine identity is something strange, built by the man's gaze. The woman is not herself, but the other in relation to the man, his object. The relationship between the two sexes is not a relationship of mutual recognition, in which the two consciousnesses relativize each other. Therefore, the woman is only the second sex: between the sexes, there is a hierarchy. The man builds his freedom in the relationship with the other, who is the woman. The woman does not build her freedom, because the man is not presented as her other, and she cannot get out of her position as an object. She remains entangled in biology, a prisoner of the species, and at the mercy of cultural constructions on the essence of the feminine.

The denial of the biological foundation of being a woman, despite being denied in different ways, is a majority in feminism, as well as the identification of the character attributed to the woman by male thought. One can see in Beauvoir's approach a remarkable example of the deconstruction of identity, as well as a philosophical structure of existentialist origin, which focuses on the issue of freedom, to which different forms of feminism converge. Freedom is considered not as a sum of rights or opportunities, but as an autonomous and original way of defining your being in the world by itself, based on your foundation.[26] This is expressed in an excerpt from this French author's account of her life with Sartre, which was widely spread: "Nothing, therefore, limited us, nothing defined us, nothing subjected us; we created them our connections with the world; freedom was our own substance."[27] From there, an existentialist motto was coined: "Let nothing define us. Let nothing subject us. Let freedom be our own substance!"

New reflections arise creating problems for sexual differences and social roles, such as the concept of gender, which does not come from grammar and linguistics. Beginning in the 1950s, John Money, a psychologist and sexologist based in the United States, uses this concept in the study of sexual reassignment of intersex people. In this case, he asks himself: if these people were born with ambiguous genitalia, how is it possible that genitalia are a decisive factor in the constitution of gender? It cannot be. So, he uses this concept to designate the result of the "gender reorientation" treatment of intersex people. John Money unties genital gender.[28] For him, sex is the organic/genetic component and gender is what people become socially, including feeling male or female in a convinced and convincing way and thus identifying for themselves and others.

Decades later, on the theoretical path opened by feminism, *queer theory* emerges to deal with sexual and gender diversity. The term *queer* comes from English and means weird or extravagant. It is a form of cursing directed at homosexuals and transgenders, which corresponds to the Portuguese *veado* or *bicha louca*. Activists and researchers appropriated this term as a form of affirmation, giving it positive content. Queer studies/activism criticize gender (male versus female) and sexual (heterosexual versus homosexual) binarism, denaturalizing collective and individual bioidentities. Such identities would have nothing natural, neural, hormonal, or idyllic. Emphasis is given to power relations to interpret the subjective and objective structures of social life and to prioritize the dimension of human protagonism in the subject's action.

According to Berenice Bento, queer studies/activism wants, in some way, to look at any guardian of morality and say:

> I no longer desire your desire. What you offer me is little. That's right, I'm queer, I'm a dyke, I'm a tranny. And what will you do with me? I am here and I will no longer live a miserable and precarious life. I want a life where I am extravagant, fuck who I want, own my own body, spit on marriage as the appropriate and unique institution to live

love and affection and vomit all the garbage you made me swallow silently.[29]

This theoretical and activist current is linked to a strong crisis of modernity that some scholars call postmodernity. A different kind of structural change has been transforming modern societies since the late twentieth century. This change fragments the cultural landscapes of class, gender, sexuality, ethnicity, race, and nationality that in the past had provided subjects with solid locations as social individuals. These transformations also change personal identities, shaking the idea that the person has an integrated subject of themself. The "subject" of the Enlightenment, who supposedly had a fixed and stable identity, was decentralized. This resulted in the open, contradictory, unfinished, and fragmented identities of the postmodern subject.[30]

Currently, the North American philosopher Judith Butler articulates feminism and sexual and gender diversity from the queer perspective. She is the author of the book *Gender Trouble: Feminism and the Subversion of Identity*. For her, gender establishes intersections with racial, classist, ethnic, sexual, and regional modalities of discursively constituted identities. It has become impossible to separate the notion of gender from the political and cultural intersections in which it is produced and maintained. Coherence and continuity of relationships between sex, gender, desire, and sexual practice are established. Causal or expressive lines of connection between biological sex, culturally constituted gender, and the expression or effect of both in the manifestation of sexual desire through sexual practice are established.[31]

The appearance of a permanent substance or an "I" with gender traits, is produced by the regulation of attributes according to lines of culturally established coherence. For Butler, there is no gender identity behind gender expressions. This identity is performatively constituted through the expressions taken as its results.[32] A statement is performative when it performs an action when pronounced, such as the yes of the spouses at the time of the marriage or "I declare the session open," so that word and act coincide. Gender identity occurs only in its expression.

The view of gender as a substance supposedly has political reasons. The institution of compulsory and naturalized heterosexuality requires and regulates gender as a binary relationship, in which the male differs from the female through practices of heterosexual desire.

The differentiation of the poles of the binary structure results in its consolidation, with the respective internal coherence of sex, gender, and desire.[33] The author proposes a twist in these configurations and their connections. What happens to the subject and the stability of gender categories as the epistemological regime of the presumption of heterosexuality is unmasked, making itself explicit as a producer and reifier of ontological categories? What is the best way to problematize the gender categories that support their hierarchy and compulsory heterosexuality?[34]

The loss of gender norms would have the effect of proliferating gender settings, destabilizing substantive identities, and stripping naturalizing narratives of the compulsory heterosexuality of their central protagonists: "men" and "women." New possibilities are sought to challenge the rigid codes of hierarchical binaries.[35] The author clarifies that her initial emphasis on denaturalization was not so much an opposition to nature as an opposition to the invocation of nature as a way of establishing necessary limits to life organized by gender.[36] The challenge is to find a better vocabulary for ways to live with gender and sexuality that don't fit so easily into the binary norm. There is a need to issue the word in which the existing complexity can be recognized, where the fear of marginalization, pathologization, and violence is radically eliminated. Butler risks saying that it may not be so important to produce new gender formulations, but rather to build a world in which people can live and breathe within their own sexuality and their own gender.[37]

Often queer reflections bring more questions than answers, more provocations than conclusions, with the permanent desire to destabilize and undermine traditional certainties in the field of gender and sexuality, as well as the resulting social practices. An example of these queer-inspired provocations is the Questionnaire for Heterosexuals[38] that was once distributed in a Spanish school to fourteen-year-olds. It questions heterosexuality as the only legitimate sexual orientation. Here are the questions:

1. What do you think caused your heterosexuality?
2. When and how did you decide you were straight?
3. Is it possible that heterosexuality is just a phase you can overcome?

4. Is it possible that your heterosexuality stems from a neurotic fear of people of your own sex?
5. If you have never had sex with a person of your own sex, isn't it possible that what you need is a good lover of your own sex?

...

8. Why do you insist on flaunting your heterosexuality? Why can't you just be who you are and be chilled?

...

10. There seem to be very few happy heterosexuals. Techniques have been developed that can help you change. Have you considered doing reversal therapy?
11. Considering the threat of starvation and overpopulation, could the human race survive if everyone was heterosexual like you?

The emergence of sexual and gender diversity also brings new identity configurations beyond the acronym LGBT. In this context, there are several types of people: intersex persons, mentioned above, showing variations of sexual characters, including chromosomes or genitals that make it difficult to identify them as fully female or male; asexual persons, supposedly born without the desire to maintain sexual relations and in some cases, neither loving relationships; pansexual persons, with sexual or loving attraction regardless of sex or gender identity; and nonbinary persons (genderqueer) who do not identify as men or women, but as something between the sexes, or a combination of both or something beyond, reacting to stereotypes and the binary system. Some extend the acronym LGBT to LGBTQ+, as in this book, where Q corresponds to nonbinary (genderqueer), and + corresponds to all other identities not included in the previous letters.

Gender studies, which cover this complexity, are known in English as gender theory. But in this case, "theory" is not an appropriate translation because these studies are quite heterogeneous. There is no unifying and comprehensive explanation, as is the case with a theory. But there is a general agreement in considering the complex behaviors, directly or indirectly linked to the sexual sphere, as the fruit of different dimensions that are not completely independent and complex: the anatomical sex, the recognition of oneself as a man or woman, gender role and sexual orientation. There is not always a necessary coherence between the sex assigned at birth, the recognition and experience of one's own identity as a man or woman, sexual desire, and sexual practice. The different identities that make up the acronym LGBTQ+ show this and express the complex diversity between men and women. Such is the common denominator of gender studies. Therefore, since there is no theory, it is advisable to talk about studies.

Such diversity and its new configurations currently benefit from the predominant human rights thinking and activism. We aspire for a world without racism, sexism, homophobia, transphobia, and any other similar discrimination.

3

THE CATHOLIC SPHERE AND THE GENDER AND SEXUAL-ORIENTATION ISSUES

AFFIRMATIONS

The change of mentality and the conquest of the rights of the LGBTQ+ population took place in nations with a majority Christian—Catholic or Protestant—population that had been deeply transformed by modern culture. Many agents of these transformations have secular motivations, expressed in nonreligious form. But there are also religious pioneering Christians, albeit a minority, whose stance contrasted strongly with other Christians or even with other faithful of their own churches.

Not everything started with Stonewall in 1969. A year earlier in the United States, Reverend Troy Perry founded the Metropolitan Community Church. He created the motto: "The Lord is my shepherd. He knows I am gay." Since then, a phrase of the Psalm, so well-known in the Christian milieu, is read from an inclusive perspective. In early 1969, Augustinian priest Patrick Nidorf founded the Catholic group Dignity USA, intended for the gay and lesbian faithful.

Surprisingly, in Brazil there is also a Christian pioneer who defended homosexuals before Stonewall, acting in the field of theology and pastoral. He is the Dutch Redemptorist priest Jaime Snoek (1920–2013), who had lived in the country since 1953. He wrote an article in the journal *Revista Vozes* of the Franciscans of Petropolis: "They are also of our lineage: considerations about homophilia."[1] It was a time when homosexuality was still considered a disease, doctors even proposed its treatment with electric shock, many countries criminalized homosexual practice, and homophobia was much greater.

This Redemptorist denounced the taboo and social censorship on this subject, about which almost no one spoke because many considered homosexuals as degenerates, perverse, and criminals. This generated a spontaneous and widespread repulsion, resulting in a conspiracy of silence. Homosexuals were ostracized and lived in the shadows, suffering bitter rejection by men and a "supposed reprobation by God." This experience makes suicide five times more frequent in homosexuals than in heterosexuals.

The hetero or homo structure is already fixed before the age of six and does not depend on the person's free choice. The prospects for therapy to change this structure are downright discouraging. The homosexual person will have to live with their condition. And there must also be for them a way of holiness, a Christian way of being homosexual. Snoek quotes the New Catechism, published by the Dutch bishops after the Second Vatican Council in 1966. This Catechism states that the stern expressions of Scripture concerning genital homosexuality should not be misunderstood, as if they denounce the fact that certain persons have same-sex attraction without fault of their own.

On the morality of the homosexual practice, Snoek formulates the question in another way: Can this experience on the erotic and genital plane promote or not the people involved in terms of oblative love, mutual interaction, humanity, and common responsibility in the construction of the world? If these values can be fulfilled, one should not a priori qualify homosexual conduct as immoral and against nature. To those who propose celibacy as a path, this is a gift and vocation; it cannot be required. It would often be infeasible.

After outlining a good overview of the theme, the article ends with five practical guidelines of the Netherlands Pastoral Institute: (1) under no circumstances can an existing friendship be broken; (2) marriage (understood as a union between man and woman) cannot be a solution and should be discouraged; (3) it should not be forgotten that continence, the so-called royal road, is not such an obvious requirement; it is observed only sporadically; (4) it seems advisable to help the homosexual to build a firm friendship; (5) in accompanying homosexual friendships, it seems important to insist above all on fidelity.

These positions, of course, were not shared by most of the Catholic world. Already at the time, the apostolic nuncio of Brazil, Dom Sebastiano Baggio, went to Petropolis and complained about Snoek's article. Baggio even said that he agreed with the content, but that the theme did not look good in a Catholic magazine.[2]

Another example of Christian pioneering in favor of LGBTQ+ is U.S. President Barack Obama, at the inauguration ceremony of his second presidential term in 2013. He was elected by many Protestants, Catholics, and Jews who went to the polls. And he took his presidential oath on the Bibles that belonged to Abraham Lincoln and Martin Luther King Jr. His inaugural address resonated with the headline: "Equality for gays and immigrants." Obama cited the Declaration of Independence of the United States of 1776, which, as noted in the previous chapter, affirms as evident truth "that all men are created equal, and are given by the Creator inalienable rights, including the right to life, freedom, and the pursuit of happiness." It is necessary to be equal not only in the eyes of God but in the eyes of men, the president continued. And this equality is a star that guides the people in the present, as it guided its ancestors in Seneca Falls, Selma, and Stonewall. The task of this generation is not complete, he says, until "our gay brothers and sisters are treated like anyone else under the law. for if we are truly created equal, then surely the love we commit to one another must be equal as well."[3]

The places he mentioned are historical icons of social struggles. Seneca Falls is the site of the first American convention in favor of female emancipation in 1848; Selma is the town in Alabama from which the Black Civil Rights marches departed in 1965, led by Martin Luther King Jr.; and Stonewall, mentioned earlier, is the gay and transgender bar in New York, where a rebellion broke out in 1969 against the discrimination and humiliation suffered by them. The equality desired by God is achieved through social movements and struggles.

The choice of the Bibles of Abraham Lincoln and Martin Luther King Jr. was not by chance. Both fought to the death for the emancipation of Blacks in their country. In the sacred book of Christians, they found inspiration and encouragement for their libertarian struggle. This was not simple. The Bible has several passages that mention slavery and segregation, and that have historically been used to justify them. Lincoln and King were not shackled to literal and fundamentalist interpretations, which were ideological weapons of their opponents. The sacred book also has other passages in favor of the submission of women to men and the prohibition of same-sex sexual relations. Even today, these passages are used by some Christians to subordinate women and to execrate LGBTQ+ people. Obama also did not submit to these interpretations. After swearing on the Bibles and referring to the Creator God, he eloquently defended Blacks, women, gays, immigrants, the poor, children, and the preservation of the planet.

Same-sex marriage was regulated in some states. In 2015, by a United States Supreme Court decision, this marriage took effect throughout the nation. There were four cases of cohabitation of same-sex unions that appealed to this court, motivating the decision. One of these unions is formed by Michael DeLeon and Greg Bourke, together for thirty-three years and with two adopted children. They are practicing Catholics and active parishioners in Louisville, Kentucky. And six of the nine Supreme Court judges were Catholics.[4]

In France, a law was passed in 2012 recognizing same-sex marriage, called Marriage for All. Society has become quite polarized, with numerous demonstrations both against and in favor. Forty percent of Catholics were in favor, among them the very author of the bill, the socialist deputy Erwann Binet. He is a practicing Catholic and saw no contradiction between his party's Christian tradition and humanitarian ideals that included the legalization of gay marriage.[5]

Marriage for All was supported by the French Catholic newspaper *Témoignage Chrétien*. This newspaper has played an important historical role since the resistance to Nazism in occupied France during World War II. It was founded in Lyon in 1941. Later, it was also in favor of European decolonization in Africa and Asia and engaged in social movements. *Témoignage Chrétien* considers itself resolutely faithful to the Second Vatican Council and its ecumenical vision, supports healthy secularism, and seeks to witness what humanizes or dehumanizes in historical happenings.

For this newspaper, homosexuality, persecuted or oppressed for centuries, is a sexual orientation as legitimate and dignified as heterosexuality. Today, civil marriage is a contract chosen by people as free and voluntary as they have ever been. To refuse this contract to homosexuals would be to add yet another discrimination to those who often already suffer countless discriminations. Therefore, it is considered fair to grant it to those who want greater legitimacy of their union. Religions must reflect on the religious sense of marriage, but it would be a serious political mistake to pit homosexuals against religious people. Marriage for All will not dissolve society. Divorce did not make marriage disappear. Many divorcees remarry. This expansion of access to marriage is a supplementary way of integration into society. There is no reason to hesitate. Humanity is magnified when citizens refuse to sacralize the bonds of blood and give priority to the bonds of fraternity that unite them. What unites them, even within the family, goes beyond the blood. Christ on the cross said to John: "Behold thy mother" and to his mother: "Woman, behold thy son." It is not biological paternity; it is not blood ties that make us brothers and sisters. Our unique and common DNA is a fraternal love, which always drives away our prejudices and fears.[6]

In the Christian world, not infrequently passages of the Bible are used to vehemently condemn LGBTQ+ people, without proper contextualization of biblical passages and the necessary consideration of the people involved. It's what Americans call "Bible bullets." But this literal use has been disputed. A letter is circulating on social media, in an ironic tone, from a Boston theology student to a radio host in the United States, who answers questions from listeners and often condemns homosexuality. It is known as Letter to a Fundamentalist (2007), and brings the following questions:

- I would like to sell my daughter as a slave, as is permitted in Exodus 21:7. What do you think would be a fair price for her nowadays?
- Leviticus 25:44 states that I can possess slaves, both men and women if they are bought from neighboring nations. A friend of mine says this applies to Mexicans, but not Canadians. Can you clarify that? Why can't I own Canadians?
- I have a neighbor who insists on working on Saturdays. Exodus 35:2 clearly states that he must be killed. Am I morally obligated to kill him myself?
- A friend of mine thinks that even if eating mollusks is an abomination (Lev 11:10), it is a lesser abomination than homosexuality. I disagree. Can you clarify that point?

- Most of my male friends trim their beards, including their temple hair, even though this is expressly forbidden in Leviticus 19:27. How should they die?

The author of the letter wants to denounce the selective use of the Bible, especially the Law of Moses, by many Jews and Christians. Slavery, the death penalty to those who work on Saturdays or trim their beards, the abomination of eating mollusks, all this is mitigated today without the slightest problem, but not homosexuality.

THE CATHOLIC HIERARCHY: RESISTANCES AND ACCEPTANCE

The major segment of the Christian world, represented by the Catholic Church, has an authorized office of teaching exercised by its hierarchy known as the magisterium. The teaching of the Church at the universal level may come from ecumenical councils presided over by the pope, from the pope himself directly, or from organs of the Roman Curia to whom he delegates.

Regarding homosexuality, the Church teaches in its *Catechism* that several men and women have deeply rooted homosexual tendencies. This inclination is "objectively disordered" and, for the majority, constitutes a trial. All of them must be welcomed with respect, compassion, and delicacy, avoiding all unjust discrimination. These people are called to do the will of God in their lives and, if they are Christians, to join in the sacrifice of the Lord's cross the difficulties they may encounter because of their condition. Based on the Bible, which presents acts of homosexuality as grave depravities (cf. Gen 19:1–29; Rom 1:24–27; 1 Cor 6:10; 1 Tim 1:10), tradition has always regarded them as "intrinsically disorderly." Such acts are contrary to natural law, close sexual intercourse to the gift of life, and do not proceed from a true affective and sexual complementarity. Under no circumstances can they be approved. Homosexuals are called to a life of chastity. By the virtues of self-control that educate inner freedom through prayer, sacramental grace, and sometimes through the support of a disinterested friendship, these people can and must gradually and resolutely approach Christian perfection (CCC, 1997, n. 2357–59).

There is also an indirect allusion to homosexual acts, mentioning that "the catechetical tradition also recalls that there are 'sins that cry to heaven': the blood of Abel, the sin of the Sodomites, the cry of the people oppressed in Egypt, the cry of the foreigner, the widow, and the orphan, injustice to the wage earner" (CCC, 1997, n. 1867).

The Church recognizes that human beings, created in the image and likeness of God, cannot be defined simply by reference to their sexual orientation. They are more than that. Every person in this world faces problems and difficulties but also has opportunities for growth, resources, talents, and gifts of their own. No human being is a mere homosexual or heterosexual. They are, above all, creatures of God and recipients of His grace, which makes them His children and heir to eternal life. All physical or verbal violence against homosexual persons is deplorable and deserving of the condemnation of the pastors of the Church wherever it occurs. There must be prudence in judgment on guilt concerning acts of homosexuality. Certain cases are recognized in which the homosexual tendency is not the fruit of the person's deliberate choice, and that this person has no alternative and is compelled to behave in a homosexual manner. Therefore, in such a situation they act without fault. There is a risk of generalizations, but there may be circumstances that reduce or even eliminate the person's guilt.[7]

Transsexuality is not explicitly mentioned in the doctrinal documents, but the teaching is that it is up to each person, man and woman, to recognize and accept their sexual identity (CCC, 1997, n. 2333). In 2015, the Congregation for the Doctrine of Faith was consulted by a Spanish bishop on the possibility of a transsexual being a godfather of baptism. The answer was that transsexual behavior publicly reveals an attitude opposed to the "moral demand to solve one's own problem of sexual identity according to the truth of one's own sex." So, this person does not fulfill the requirement to live a life according to faith and the role of godfather.[8]

During the pontificate of John Paul II, when the restrictions on homosexuality were well evidenced, there was also the question of possible "just discrimination" against gays and lesbians. The Roman Curia asserted that "sexual tendency" is not a characteristic comparable to race or ethnic traditions concerning nondiscrimination. The homosexual tendency is an objective disorder and requires moral solicitude. There is no right to homosexuality. It is fair to consider the sexual tendency in the adoption and custody of children, in the admission of teachers or sports coaches, and in military recruitment. Human rights are not absolute. They can be legitimately limited due to "objective disorder of external conduct." This is lawful and sometimes necessary not only in the case of voluntary behavior but also in cases of physical or mental illness. The state may restrict rights, for example in the case of mental or contagious illness, to protect the common good.[9] Non-discrimination of gays and lesbians is only a right insofar as there is no homoerotic conduct. Otherwise, discrimination may be legitimate for the protection of the common good.

The Church strongly opposed the legal recognition of homosexual unions. For the Church, these unions do not perform—not even in a remote analog way—the functions for which marriage (heterosexual) and the family deserve specific and qualified recognition. There are reasons to say that such unions are "harmful to the correct progress of human society." Faced with the recognition or equality of homosexual unions with marriage, with access to the rights proper to the latter, it is necessary to oppose clearly and incisively. Any formal and material cooperation in the promulgation and application of these laws should be avoided and, as far as possible, the conscientious objection should be used. There was, however, a concession. Although with caveats, it is stated that in the case of homosexual people living together can recognize rights with legal protection for situations of mutual interest. But on the insertion of children in homosexual unions, there are no concessions. It should be avoided because it lacks the sexual bipolarity provided by paternity and motherhood. This creates obstacles to the normal development of children.[10]

There is also strong opposition from the Catholic hierarchy and other Christian segments to certain fields of gender studies, as well as to the activism that stems from them. These studies are the main theoretical elements of those who defend equality between men and women in society, and the inclusion and LGBTQ+ citizenship. In the public space, this opposition generates disputes in the elaboration and implementation of laws and public policies involving family, education, health, and rights.

According to the Roman Curia, the threats to the family are due to the exaltation of liberal individualism, combined with a subjective ethic of the unbridled pursuit of pleasure, with new expressions of Marxist-inspired socialism. A trend that was manifested at the Beijing Conference in 1995 aimed to introduce "gender ideology" to the people. For this ideology, the greatest form of oppression of men over women is the institutionalized monogamous family, founded on a heterosexual union. The roles of men and women in society are mere products of history and culture. It is appropriate to end this family model so that the woman is free from oppression. And as for sexual orientation, human beings are free to choose what pleases them, whatever may be their biological sex.[11] The term *gender ideology* first appears in a normative document of the Roman Curia. It will then have wide diffusion, referring to the set of propositions considered unacceptable concerning gender identity and sexual orientation.

The alert against theoretical trends arising from the theme of women continued. To avoid any supremacy of one sex over the other, one tends to "eliminate their differences" considering them as mere effects of historical-cultural conditioning. The bodily difference, called sex, is minimized; and the cultural dimension, called gender, is maximized, and considered primary. Such anthropology obscures the duality of the sexes in favor of egalitarian perspectives for the woman; questions the biparental nature of the family, composed of father and mother; and equates homosexuality to heterosexuality in a new model of polymorphic sexuality. The deepest motivation for this tendency would be in the attempt of the human person to "free himself from his own biological conditioning." Human nature would not have characteristics that impose themselves absolutely, but each person could and should model themselves to their liking, free from all predetermination linked to their essential constitution. In the face of such currents of thought, one must react by drawing inspiration from faith in Jesus Christ. Instead of antagonism and the elimination of the difference between men and women, it proposes active collaboration based on the recognition of this very difference.[12]

The tone of criticism of gender studies rose during the pontificate of Benedict XVI. For him, faith in the Creator is an essential part of the Christian creed, and the Catholic Church should not limit itself to transmitting to the faithful the message of salvation alone. The Church also has a responsibility toward creation. It must defend the gifts of creation that belong to all and protect human beings against self-destruction. There must be a human ecology. The nature of the human being as man and woman is not an outdated metaphysics. It is about faith in the Creator and listening to the language of creation, whose contempt would mean a "self-destruction" of the human being and a destruction of God's own work. The Pope continues to say:

> What is often expressed and understood by the term "gender" ultimately ends up being man's attempt at self-emancipation from creation and the Creator. Man wants to be his own master, and alone—always and exclusively—to determine everything that concerns him. Yet in this way he lives in opposition to the truth, in opposition to the Creator Spirit.
>
> Rain forests deserve indeed to be protected, but no less so does man, as a creature having an innate "message" which does not contradict our freedom, but is instead its very premise.[13]

The Church's teachings on homosexuals and their unions were openly contested by a section of the Chicago clergy. In the name of the dignity of the human person and the respect due to them, these priests criticized the "demonization" of gays and lesbians and the tone of such violence and abuse against them who are children of God and the Church. No one except them would be slaughtered by such a "vile" language. Expressions such as intrinsically disordered, harmful unions, serious depravities, legalization of evil, and serious damage to the common good, are a bombardment that destroys self-respect and self-esteem in many. This "disgusting and toxic language" forces them to abandon active participation in the Church and to question how they can remain in an institution they experience as abusive. It is not possible to work pastorally on the needs of homosexual people based on this kind of language. The priests propose a new atmosphere of open dialogue that includes the lived experience of the faithful, recognizing the divine blessing in the lives of countless homosexuals in their relationships, and that their experiences be heard with respect.[14]

Despite strong criticism of gender studies and the legalization of gay marriage, there has been a breakthrough in the decriminalization of homosexuality. At the end of 2008, a proposal was presented at the United Nations (U.N.) headed by France in favor of this decriminalization worldwide. The proposal included an end to discrimination based on sexual orientation and gender identity. At the time, according to human rights groups, homoerotism was punishable in more than ninety countries and could lead to the death penalty in Afghanistan, Iran, Saudi Arabia, Sudan, and Yemen. The French proposal generated a heated debate and had the accession of sixty-six countries and the rejection of fifty-seven. The latter, led by Egypt, presented a statement of opposition.

At the U.N., the Holy See delegation expressed appreciation for the French proposal to condemn all forms of violence against homosexuals, and urged states, including Muslims, to take the necessary steps to end all criminal penalties against them.[15] For the Church, freely consented sexual relations between adult persons should not be considered a civil offense. But the Holy See opposed the end of discrimination by gender identity and sexual orientation. It claimed that this could become an instrument of pressure against those who consider homosexual behavior morally unacceptable, do not recognize a homosexual union as a family, its equivalence to a heterosexual union, and its right to adoption and assisted reproduction.[16]

The position of the Catholic Church leadership in favor of the decriminalization of homosexuality worldwide did not have many repercussions at the time, but in the historical horizon, this means a huge change. The Church—which in the past tried and condemned homosexuals, then called Sodomites—went on to urge all nations, even Muslims, to eliminate all criminal measures against them. Defending that free sexual acts among adult persons are not considered a crime by civil authority is the position of the Enlightenment and the Napoleonic Code. This position even clashes with the pontificate of John Paul II, whose doctrinal documents affirm that there are no rights to homosexuality, that human rights can be restricted by the state in case of objective disorder of external conduct, and that homosexual unions are harmful to society. This could precisely justify the criminalization of homosexuality. Curiously, these documents came from the Congregation for the Doctrine of Faith, directed by the late Cardinal Ratzinger. But as a pope, no longer under the orders of his predecessor, he had more freedom and walked another path.

EPISCOPAL CONFERENCES

In the Catholic hierarchy, in addition to the teachings of popes and the Roman Curia, the episcopal conferences, through their documents, bring important contributions to theology and pastoral ministries that are the fruit of their reflection and practice contextualized in different realities. Because they are teachings at a regional, national, or even continental level, there may be appropriate and timely reflections and proposals that do not appear in documents of universal scope.

The North American bishops have experience with pastoral ministry with homosexuals. Those who work in this field are invited to listen to the experiences, needs, and hopes of homosexuals. This shows respect for the innate dignity and conscience of the other. Gays and lesbians can reveal their condition to family and friends and grow up in the Christian life. The bishops do not approve of the adoption of children by same-sex couples. However, they accept the baptism of children under the responsibility of these couples, if there is a purpose for them to be educated in the faith of the Catholic Church.[17]

There is also a beautiful letter from the North American bishops addressed to the parents of homosexuals, whose title is prophetic: "Always Our Children." The bishops say that God does not love a person less because they are gay or lesbian. AIDS may not be a divine punishment. God is much more powerful, more compassionate, and, if need be, more forgiving than anyone in this world. Parents are urged to love themselves and not to blame themselves for their children's sexual orientation or their choices. Parents are not required to refer their children to reversal therapies to make them heterosexual. Parents are encouraged to show them unconditional love. And depending on the situation of the children, family support is even more necessary.[18] There are many families in other countries who have homosexual children and suffer greatly from this. Parents often blame themselves and do not know what to do. This message is very necessary also in other ecclesial and family realities.

The blessing of homosexuals was dealt with by the Swiss bishops. They claim that they can be blessed, but not the contraction of a same-sex union so that there is no resemblance to sacramental marriage.[19] With this, other possibilities arise. In the Rite of Blessings of the Church, for example, there is a blessing of a residence, with prayers for those who reside in it, a blessing of the workplace, and blessings for various circumstances. Therefore, one can bless homosexual persons without contradicting Church norms. In the search for practices that favor reception, these are timely initiatives.

When the Marriage for All Act was voted in France, the French bishops opposed the equality of homosexual union with the heterosexual union. Nevertheless, they repudiated homophobia and congratulated the evolution of the law that today condemns all discrimination and incitement to hatred on grounds of sexual orientation. They recognize that it is often not easy for the homosexual person to assume their condition because prejudices are lasting and mentalities only change slowly, even in Catholic communities and families. These are called to welcome every person as a child of God, whatever their situation may be. And, in a lasting union between people of the same sex, beyond the purely sexual aspect, the Church esteems the value of solidarity, sincere connection, attention, and care for the other.[20] This pronouncement takes important steps, as it honors civil legislation against discrimination and brings a positive outlook to homoaffective unions.

The Brazilian bishops included this theme when dealing with the pastoral renewal of parishes. With realism and openness, they recognized new family situations, including same-sex unions. They observe that people united without the sacramental bond and others in second unions participate in the parishes. Some live alone supporting their children, grandparents who raise grandchildren, and uncles and aunts who provide for nephews and nieces. There are children adopted by single or same-sex people, who live in a stable union. They urge the Church, the family of Christ, to welcome all its children with love. In keeping with Christian teaching about the family, it is necessary to use mercy. Many have moved away and continue to move away from communities because they felt rejected when the first response they received was prohibitions instead of living the faith amid difficulties. There must be pastoral conversion in parish renewal so as not to empty the good news proclaimed by the Church and, at the same time, not to neglect the new situations of family life. "Welcome, guide and include" in communities those living in other family settings, these are pressing challenges.[21]

Regarding education, the British bishops produced and disseminated in the schools of their dioceses a good manual for confronting bullying based on homophobia, biphobia, and transphobia.[22] Bullying is the practice of acts of physical or verbal violence, intentional and repeated, against a defenseless person, and may cause them physical and psychological damage. This is very important as LGBTQ+ children and young people are often severely oppressed. It is not uncommon for school and even the family itself to become like hell for these people.

The episcopal conferences thus offer valuable elements that favor the reception and apostolate with LGBTQ+ people.

FRANCIS'S PONTIFICATE

The Catholic Church's relationship with LGBTQ+ people undeniably lives a new moment with the pontificate of Francis. When he returned from Brazil to Rome in 2013, he said something that had a lot of repercussions: "If someone is gay and is searching for the Lord and has good will, then who am I to judge him?...No one should marginalize these people for this."[23] This statement is unprecedented coming from a pope, especially for positively employing the term gay. It takes up the teaching of the Second Vatican Council on freedom and autonomy of conscience and brings it into the reality of homosexual persons.

The Pope urges the Catholic Church to live in a time of pastoral renewal. He calls on the Church to go to the "existential peripheries," to meet those who suffer from various forms of injustice, conflict, and needs. We must open ourselves to the newness that God brings to our lives, that fulfills us and gives us true joy and serenity because God loves us and wants nothing but our good. He criticizes a self-sufficient Church, entrenched in "stale structures that have lost the capacity to welcome" and closed to the new paths that God presents today. For him, the action of the Holy Spirit lifts the eyes of the faithful to the horizon, impelling them to these peripheries.[24]

The renewal in this pontificate is made with pastoral openness, new doctrinal approaches, bold gestures, and the unleashing of new processes. All of this influences the relationship with the LGBTQ+. The pope's moral teaching is both nuanced, open, critical, and encouraging. He says that "the proclamation of God's saving love precedes moral and religious obligation. Today, sometimes, it seems that the reverse order prevails."[25] A missionary ministry should not be obsessed with the disjointed transmission of a multitude of doctrines to be imposed insistently, even involving topics such as abortion, homosexual marriage, and the use of contraceptive methods. Proclamation must focus on the essential, which is also the most passionate and attractive, seeking to heal every kind of wound and to touch the heart, like that of the disciples of Emmaus who found the risen Christ. The evangelical proposal must be simpler, deeper, and more radiant. It is from this proposal that the moral consequences must follow. In this perspective, the confessional is not a torture room, but a place of mercy, in which the Lord urges us to do the best we can.[26]

Salvation also has an immanent dimension because to evangelize, says the pope, is to make the kingdom of God present in this world. The Gospel invites us first to respond to God who loves and saves us, recognizing Him in others and coming out of ourselves to seek the good of all. Those who allow themselves to be saved by Christ are freed from sin, sadness, inner emptiness, and isolation. Christian moral preaching is not a Stoic ethic of the impassive fulfillment of duty, nor a catalog of sins and errors. It is more than a disciplined asceticism or conduct, and more than a practical philosophy. There is a disproportion to be avoided when speaking more of the law than of grace, more of the Church than of Jesus Christ, and more of the pope than of the word of God (cf. *Evangelii Gaudium* 1, 39, 38).

Francis also defends single mothers who want to baptize their children and face the bureaucracies created by religious rigorists. The Church should be the paternal home where there is room for all who face hardships in their lives. Everyone can participate in ecclesial life and be part of the community. The doors of the sacraments must not be closed for any reason, starting with the first: baptism. The Eucharist, the fullness of sacramental life, is not a reward for the perfect, but a generous remedy and nourishment for those who need strength. This has pastoral consequences to be considered with prudence and boldness. We often act as controllers of grace rather than facilitators. But the Church is not a tollhouse, it is the paternal house (cf. EG 47).

The knowledge of truth is progressive, notes the pope, relying on Saint Vincent of Lérins, one of the fifth-century Church fathers. Human beings' understanding changes over time, Francis continues, and their consciousness deepens. We remember the time when slavery was accepted, and the death penalty was admitted without any problem. Exegetes and theologians, as well as other sciences and their evolution, helped the Church to mature its own judgment. Consequently, some secondary ecclesial norms and precepts were once effective, but today have lost value or meaning. A view of the doctrine of the Church as a monolithic block to be defended without nuances is wrong.[27]

He did not list all the secondary norms and precepts, which have lost their value amid the evolution of theology and sciences, because this process is dynamic, involves ecclesial consensus, and always articulates permanence and change. But the pope points to theology and the evolution of sciences as agents of the Church's maturation. This is based on the teaching of the Second Vatican Council. What the apostles of Jesus transmitted to the Church progresses under the assistance of the Holy Spirit. Throughout the centuries, the Church continually strives toward the fullness of divine truth (cf. DV 8). Theology and the profane sciences lead the faithful to a purer and more adult life of faith (cf. GS 62). There is an order or hierarchy of truths in Catholic doctrine, according to the nexus of these truths with the foundation of the Christian faith. Some points are more important because they are closely linked to this foundation. Others, in turn, are less important because they are less connected to it (UR 11). When the *Catechism of the Catholic Church* was twenty-five years old, the pope reiterated the dynamic and progressive aspect of the Church's teaching: "Doctrine cannot be preserved without allowing it to develop, nor can it be tied to an interpretation that is rigid and immutable without demeaning the working of the Holy Spirit."[28]

The hierarchy of truths is valid, says the pope, both for the dogmas of faith and for the other teachings of the Church, including moral doctrine. In the moral message, there is a hierarchy of virtues and actions. Mercy is the greatest of virtues. The works of love for the neighbor are the most perfect outward manifestation of the Spirit's inward grace. The precepts given by Christ and the apostles to the people of God are very few. And the precepts added later by the Church must be demanded in moderation, not to make life heavy for the faithful and not to transform religion into slavery (cf. EG 36–37, 43).

In this nuanced morality that the pope exposes, the possible good is of great importance. Without diminishing the value of the evangelical ideal, it is necessary to accompany, with mercy and patience, the possible stages of the person's growth, which is built day by day. A small step amid great human limitations can be more pleasing to God than an outwardly correct life of those who do not face great difficulty. The consolation and strength of God's saving love must reach everyone. God works mysteriously in every person, beyond their defects and failings. A missionary heart does not renounce the good possible, even if it runs the risk of getting dirty with the mud of the road (cf. EG 44–45).

An example of the relationship between the evangelical ideal and the possible good is the family formed by the exclusive and indissoluble union between a man and a woman. All popes defend this institution. But Francis once made an interesting and unexpected compliment to the Paraguayan women, whom he considers "the most glorious in Latin America." This is because after the Paraguayan War—against Brazil, Argentina, and Uruguay between 1864 and 1870—eight women remained in Paraguay for each man. And Paraguayan women made a difficult and risky choice: to have children to save their homeland, culture, faith, and language.[29] The pope praised an extramarital practice of procreation, done on a national scale in extreme circumstances. These women are considered more glorious than all others, including those who live in the traditional family model. With this, Francis does not contradict Catholic morality and does not diminish his appreciation of marriage, but courageously shows the broad scope of the search for the possible good in the field of morality.

Graduality in the application of moral law is not a new element in doctrine, including what concerns chastity. The search for the possible good often impels the faithful to tread a progressive path of growth in stages through phases marked by imperfection and even sin, as the *Catechism* teaches.[30] But this graduality is almost unknown in many Catholic settings and should be taught more broadly. Often there is a triumph of all or nothing, of sterile idealism without patience and mercy. The pope is adamant against this rigidity: "Stay away! They bite you!"[31]

The novelty of his pontificate concerning the LGBTQ+ goes beyond magisterial documents. It is also in positive and inspiring examples of public gestures and words in welcoming these people. In early 2015, he received at his home the visit of the Spanish transsexual Diego Neria and his companion Macarena, letting himself be photographed with both. Diego's life story then became known, showing the atrocious prejudice that many transgender people suffer and how to face it.

He was born with female genitalia, but as a child, he felt like a man. His brain and self-perception did not correspond to the rest of the body. At Christmas, Diego wrote to the Magi asking as a gift to become a boy. Growing up, he resigned himself to his condition. "My prison was my own body because it did not correspond absolutely to what my soul felt," he confesses. He hid this reality as much as he could. His mother asked him not to change his body while she lived. And he accepted this wish until her death. When she died, Diego was thirty-nine years old. A year later, he began the transitioning process. In the church he used to attend, people were aroused: "How dare you enter here in your condition? You are not worthy." Once, he heard from a priest in the street: "You are the devil's daughter!" But fortunately, he had the support of the bishop of his diocese, who gave him courage and comfort. This encouraged Diego to write to Pope Francis and ask for a meeting with him. The pope welcomed him and embraced him in the Vatican, in the presence of his companion, with words that brought him great comfort. Today, Diego Neria is a man at peace.[32]

In the United States, Francis received in the apostolic nunciature his former student and gay friend Yayo Grassi and his companion. Grassi had already introduced his companion to the pope two years earlier. This relationship was never a problem in the friendship between Grassi and Francis. Also, the Chilean Juan Carlos Cruz, a victim of sexual abuse by a priest, was received by the pontiff, with whom he spoke at length. Francis told him, "Juan Carlos, that you're gay doesn't matter. God made you that way and loves you that way, and I don't care. The Pope loves you that way. You need to be happy as you are"—as reported by Juan Carlos Cruz.[33] This invaluable comment is not an official pronouncement, appearing on the Vatican website, but a private conversation of the pope.

Diego was not reprimanded by the pope for having done the transitioning process, nor for having later married a woman. Grassi and Cruz have not heard from Francis that homosexual tendencies are objectively disordered and can lead to intrinsically disordered acts, according to the *Catechism*. Nevertheless, it cannot be said that this pope despises the doctrinal documents of the Church, but in these matters, he turns to what is more pastorally important: the goodness of divine creation, the unconditional love of God, the acceptance of the person and the autonomy of their conscience. These examples show what it looks like to welcome and not judge and are worth even more than many words. If all parents and relatives of LGBTQ+ people followed the example of the pope, receiving them in their homes with their respective companions, various problems of this population would be solved.

A journalist asked Francis what he would say to a transgender person, and whether he as pastor and minister would accompany them. The pope replied that he has been accompanying homosexual and transgender people, recalling the case of Diego, and urged: "Individuals have to be accompanied, as Jesus accompanies them. [...] for every case welcome it, accompany it, look into it, discern and integrate it. This is what Jesus would do today."[34] Diego's story is not the exaltation of liberal individualism, the unbridled pursuit of pleasure, or human self-reliance that rebels against the work of the Creator. But it shows the inner truth of the person that comes out, as in the lives of so many LGBTQ+.

The opening of Francis's pontificate includes the exhortation to theologians to continue on the path of the Second Vatican Council, and to reread the Gospel from the perspective of contemporary culture. Studying and teaching theology must mean "living on a frontier," in which the Gospel meets the needs of the people to whom it is announced in an understandable and meaningful way. One should avoid a theology that runs out in academic disputes or that contemplates humanity from a glass castle. It must accompany cultural and social processes, especially difficult transitions, assuming the conflicts that affect everyone. Good theologians, like good pastors, must have "the odor of the people and of the street," and with their reflection pour "oil and wine onto the wounds of mankind," like the Good Samaritan of the Gospel.[35]

For the pope, the theologian must face the hard work of distinguishing the message of life from its form of transmission, from its cultural elements in which at a certain time it was codified. Failure to do this exercise of discernment inevitably leads to betrayal of the content of the message. It makes the good news, the true meaning of the Gospel, no longer new and no longer good, becoming a sterile word, empty of all its creative, healing, and resuscitating force. Thus, the faith of the people of our time is endangered. Christian doctrine must not be a closed system, deprived of dynamics capable of generating questions and doubts. On the contrary, it has a face, body, and flesh, which is called Jesus Christ. It is His life that is offered from generation to generation to all human beings, in all parts of the world.[36]

Gender studies are part of the pope's preaching. In public speaking, he spoke about family and the restlessness that such studies bring to him. According to the Judeo-Christian tradition, the family institution is a great gift that God gave to humanity, creating man and woman and instituting the sacrament of marriage. Sexual difference is present in various forms of life, but only in man and woman does this difference bring the image and the divine likeness. Its purpose is not opposition or subordination, but communion and generation. The human being needs reciprocity between men and women to know themself well and grow harmonically. And recently, the pope stated that culture has opened new spaces, freedoms, and depths that enrich the understanding of this difference, but it has also brought many doubts and skepticism. And he asks this question: "I ask myself, if the so-called gender theory is not, at the same time, an expression of frustration and resignation, which seeks to cancel out sexual difference because it no longer knows how to confront it."[37] For him, there is a risk of taking a step back. Removing the difference would truly be the problem, not the solution.

The pope's remarkable ecological encyclical, *Laudato Si'* (LS), also touches on gender issues. It is up to the human being to "accept our body, to care for it and to respect its fullest meaning," because this is essential for a true human ecology. The pope continues to say that "valuing one's own body in its femininity or masculinity" is necessary for proper recognition of oneself in the encounter with the other who is different (n. 155). In the horizon of this encyclical, there is something very important from a historical perspective and quite relevant in contemporary times: the refutation of dualism and contempt for the body and matter.

Jesus is pointed out as one who lived in full harmony with creation, who did not appear as an ascetic separated from the world, or even as an enemy of the pleasurable things of life. When he spoke of Himself, he said: "The Son of Man came eating and drinking, and they say, 'Look, a glutton and a drunkard'" (Matt 11:19). Jesus worked with his own hands, coming into contact daily with the matter created by God to shape it with His craftsmanship. Remarkably, most of His earthly existence was devoted to this task. Therefore, "He was far removed from philosophies which despised the body, matter and the things of the world. Such unhealthy dualisms, nonetheless, left a mark on certain Christian thinkers in the course of history and disfigured the Gospel" (LS 98). Gender and sexuality issues can be successfully rethought by refuting these dualisms.

THE SYNOD OF BISHOPS ON THE FAMILY AND ITS CONSEQUENCES

Already in the first year of Francis's pontificate, in 2013, the synod of bishops was convened to address the family and its current challenges, beginning a rich and creative period. The Christian message in the field of sexuality and the family has undeniable greatness and beauty, but also unavoidable problems and questions. At certain points, there is a noticeable disparity between the teaching of the Church and the life of the majority of the faithful. In the preparatory questionnaire to the synod that was sent to all the Catholic dioceses of the world, there was a special concern, among other things, on what pastoral attention can be given to people who have chosen to live in same-sex unions and, if they adopt children, what to do to transmit their faith. There were many debates and interviews, and extensive reports were produced, with a remarkable impact on the media.

The synod, including its reports and propositions, is an advisory institution. After its completion, the pope publishes a post-synodal exhortation, which is the official teaching (magisterium) of the Church on the subject treated. Even though it is only consultative, the synod brings very relevant indications regarding the ecclesial situation, the existing consensus, and disagreements among the bishops, which are very important for the pope's discernment.

The reports produced since the convocation of this synod clearly pointed in this direction: not to change the Church's doctrine on the family, founded on the exclusive and indissoluble union between a man and a woman, but at the same time welcome without condemning people living in other family settings. The value of this process, beyond normative texts, is the open debate in the Church on issues of sexuality, family, gender, and bioethics as never seen in recent decades. This helps to form and express the consensus of the faithful, favoring pastoral ministry, theological reflection, and the creative reception of the post-synodal exhortation that also influences the relationship between church, state, and public policy.

At the closing assembly of the synod, the pope made a very realistic assessment of the differences between the bishops:

> We have also seen that what seems normal for a bishop on one continent, is considered strange and almost scandalous—almost!—for a bishop from another; what is considered a violation of a right in one society is an evident and inviolable rule in another; what for some is freedom of conscience is for others simply confusion. Cultures are in fact quite diverse, and every general principle…needs to be inculturated, if it is to be respected and applied.[38]

The post-synodal exhortations are drawn from the consensus reached in the synodal assemblies. The magisterium of the Church at the universal level must consider the different contexts of continents and countries. The task of articulating convergences and reaching a common denominator is complex and difficult. Pope Benedict XVI reported on the mission he received when he was cardinal, in the time of John Paul II, to coordinate the work of the bishops for the preparation of the *Catechism of the Catholic Church*. The book should show what the Church believes today and how it can reasonably be believed. He confesses that he was frightened by this mission and doubted that this was feasible. How could people living on different continents, not only geographically, but also intellectually and spiritually, come to a text with internal cohesion and comprehensibility on all continents? He considers the fulfillment of this mission a prodigy.[39] Faced with the complexity of obtaining consensus and at the same time respecting differences, universal teaching does not say everything about a subject and tends to be cautious in innovations.

The pope's exhortation on the family was signed on the day of Saint Joseph (March 19, 2016), who in the Catholic liturgy is the patron of the Holy Family, composed of Jesus, Mary, and Joseph. *Amoris Laetitia* (AL) is a broad dissertation, based on the premise that the joy of love lived in families is also the joy of the Church. The strength of the family lies essentially in its ability to love and teach to love (cf. AL 1, 53). Many contemporary situations and issues are contemplated, shedding light on concrete family life. The exhortation is far from an abstract and cold doctrinal text. The great novelty lies in the strong pastoral sensitivity, with very careful nuances in the application of the doctrine. For the pope, not all doctrinal, moral, and pastoral discussions should be resolved with the intervention of the magisterium. Of course, a unity of doctrine and praxis is necessary for the Church, but this does not prevent there being different ways of interpreting some aspects of the doctrine or some consequences that arise from it. In each country or region, one can seek more enculturated solutions, attentive to local traditions and challenges (cf. AL 3).

Francis warns strongly against the moralistic impetus that often reigns in Christian circles and the hierarchy of the Catholic Church, to foster due respect for the conscience and autonomy of the faithful:

> We also find it hard to make room for the consciences of the faithful, who very often respond as best they can to the Gospel amid their limitations, and are capable of carrying out their own discernment in complex situations. We have been called to form consciences, not to replace them. (AL 37)

Along the same lines, the moral formation of the new generations must be carried out inductively, so that a son and a daughter can discover for themselves the importance of certain values, principles, and norms, instead of imposing them as indisputable truths (cf. AL 264).

In every circumstance, before those who have difficulty fully living the law of God, the invitation must resound to follow the path of charity, the path of love. Fraternal charity is the first law of Christians, according to Jesus's command: "Love one another as I have loved you" (John 15:12). It is the fullness of the law (Gal 5:14). Without diminishing the evangelical ideal, one must accompany with mercy and patience the possible stages of growth of people, which are built day by day. The Lord's mercy encourages us to do what is good (AL 306, 308). It is necessary to open our hearts to those who live in the most varied existential peripheries. Pastors are invited to listen with affection and serenity, with the sincere desire to enter the heart of people's drama and understand their point of view, to help them live better and recognize their place in the Church (cf. AL 312).

It cannot be said that all who are in a situation called irregular live in a state of mortal sin, deprived of sanctifying grace. A pastor cannot be satisfied only with the application of the moral law to those who live in this situation as if they were stones thrown at people's lives. Because of conditioning or mitigating factors, one can live in God's grace, and love, and grow in a life of grace and charity, receiving the help of the Church that includes the sacraments. Therefore, priests should be reminded that the confessional, where the sacrament of penance is commonly administered, is not a torture room, but the place of the Lord's mercy. And the Eucharist is not a prize for the perfect, but a generous remedy and food for those in need (AL 301, 305, n. 351).

The question of access to the sacraments of those living in an irregular situation, especially those divorced and remarried, has been quite controversial since the convocation of the synod. For decades, the faithful, pastors, and theologians have sought solutions to this matter. The pope does not give a definite and comprehensive solution, but he opens the way for pastors so that, in accompanying the faithful and respecting their discernment, they can minister the sacraments to them. Considerations about the faithful in an irregular situation also apply to those who live in other family settings, such as unmarried parents and same-sex unions.

The reservations of the Catholic hierarchy in recent decades about "gender ideology" are also contemplated in the final report of the synod and ratified in the post-synodal exhortation. It is stated that this ideology

> denies the difference and reciprocity in nature of a man and a woman and envisages a society without sexual differences, thereby eliminating the anthropological basis of the family. This ideology leads to educational programmes and legislative enactments that promote a personal identity and emotional intimacy radically separated from the biological difference between male and female. Consequently, human identity becomes the choice of the individual, one which can also change over time." It is a source of concern that some ideologies of this sort, which seek to respond to what are at times understandable aspirations, manage to assert themselves as absolute and unquestionable, even dictating how children should be raised. It needs to be emphasized that "biological sex and the socio-cultural role of sex (gender) can be distinguished but not separated. (AL 56)

This set of propositions called gender ideology is not defended by a specific author, but it is a grouping of statements considered unacceptable, coming from more than one author. Something similar happened with the condemnation of modernism made by the Catholic hierarchy in the early twentieth century. There was not one author who at the same time defended all the propositions that were condemned under the title of modernism.

The specific issues of homosexuality, in turn, are posed by reminding us that the Church must embody the behavior of Jesus. He offers himself to everyone without exception, with a love without borders. To families who have homosexual children, it is reaffirmed that every person, regardless of their sexual orientation, must be welcomed and respected in their dignity, avoiding all unjust discrimination, aggression, and violence. A respectful accompaniment should be assured so that all who manifest a homosexual tendency have the necessary help to understand and fully realize the will of God in their lives (cf. AL 250). The reception of homosexual persons, already taught in the *Catechism* (1997, n. 3528), is brought into the context of families with homosexual children, where this is most urgent. However, the equivalence of homosexual unions to marriage is not accepted because there is no comparison between such unions and the divine plan for marriage and the family. It is also not accepted that there is pressure from international bodies, making financial aid to poor countries conditional on the introduction of laws in this direction (cf. AL 251).

Feminism was also contemplated, with support and caveats. The same dignity between man and woman impels us to rejoice in overcoming old forms of discrimination and developing a style of reciprocity within families. If forms of feminism appear that cannot be considered adequate, the work of the Spirit is equally admired in the clearer recognition of the dignity of women and their rights (cf. AL 54). Pope Francis confesses: "I certainly value feminism, but one that does not demand uniformity or negate motherhood." Indeed, the greatness of women implies all the rights deriving from their inalienable human dignity, but also from their "feminine genius, which is essential to society" (AL 173). This expression, already used by John Paul II, refers to the specifically feminine capacities—especially motherhood—that also confers duties on women, since their being also implies a peculiar mission on this earth, that society must protect and preserve for the good of all (cf. AL 173).

After the post-synodal exhortation, gender, and sexual-orientation issues are still addressed in documents released by the Vatican. One of them is "'Male and Female He Created Them': Towards a Path of Dialogue on the Question of Gender Theory in Education."[40] It basically reiterates the Catholic Church's traditional teachings on anthropology and sexuality, including its fears. The title itself refers to the first chapters of the Bible, to the creation of man and woman, to unite for all life, procreate and populate the earth. At the same time, however, it opens some paths that may be promising.

The subtitle already proposes a bilateral dialogue in the treatment of the controversial and not rarely explosive subject of gender. The unique contribution of this document is the distinction between ideology and various research on gender carried out by the human sciences, recognizing that there is no lack of research seeking to deepen how one lives the sexual difference between men and women in different cultures adequately (n. 6). Thus, there's no reason for certain hysteria every time gender is discussed. Another positive aspect is the warning against bullying. In the education of children and young people, one must respect each one in their different and peculiar condition so that no one is a victim of violence, insults, and discrimination (n. 16).

This document does not meet the hopes of those who expected the leadership of the Catholic Church to condemn gender studies firmly, and neither does it meet the expectations of those who wanted an open and articulated debate on such studies. As this is a proposal to foster dialogue and not a definitive and unquestionable pronouncement, it is necessary to listen to the other possible partners of this dialogue. Among them are the diverse researchers and people whom they research: women and men, including heterosexuals and cisgender, as well as other LGBTQ+. Their experience and their conscience cannot be neglected.

Another document is: "'What Is Man?' (Psalm 8:5): An Itinerary through Biblical Anthropology."[41] This outlines a new understanding of same-sex unions, without condemning them, even stating that there is no example of their legal recognition in biblical tradition:

> Some time ago, particularly in Western culture, dissenting voices were expressed in relation to the anthropological approach of Scripture, as it is understood and transmitted by the Church in its normative aspects. All this is judged as a simple reflection of an archaic and historically conditioned mentality. We know that various biblical statements, in the cosmological, biological and sociological spheres, have been gradually overtaken by the progressive affirma-

> tion of the natural and human sciences; analogously—some deduce—a new and more adequate understanding of the human person imposes a radical reservation in relation to the exclusive appreciation of heterosexual union, in favour of a similar acceptance of homosexuality and homosexual unions as a legitimate and dignified expression of the human being. (n. 185)

It then deals with Bible texts used to condemn the practice of homosexuality, including those mentioned in the *Catechism* (cf. Gen 19:1–29; Rom 1:24–27; 1 Cor 6:10; 1 Tim 1:10), showing other non-condemnatory interpretations (nn. 185–95). Because it is a Vatican document that addresses this reality, the teaching makes an important contribution that situates it from the perspective of the evolution of the doctrine.

Finally, in matters of gender and sexual orientation, much remains to be done in the Catholic world to tread the path opened by the Second Vatican Council of rereading the Gospel from the perspective of contemporary culture. It should be noted that at the opening of this council, Pope John XXIII gave an energetic warning against the prophets of catastrophe who only see prevarication and ruin, always announcing unfortunate events as if the end of the world was imminent. They repeat that in our time, in comparison with the past, things only got worse; and "they behave as if they had learned nothing from history."[42] Even today there are prophets of catastrophe who stubbornly see destructive threats to the family and society. For them, it would only remain for the Catholic Church to reiterate dogmas, precepts, and prohibitions.

Pope Francis recalled the famous warning of his predecessor about such prophets and presented a positive perspective, exactly the opposite of this doomsday outlook: the eye of the believer can recognize the light of the Holy Spirit radiating in darkness, to glimpse the wine in which the water can be transformed, and to discover the wheat that grows in the middle of the chaff (cf. EG 84). The time has come to recognize this light, glimpse this wine, and discover this wheat in the paths that favor the citizenship of the LGBTQ+ population in society and the Church. So those who believe can then contribute to a world where everyone can live and breathe in their gender and sexuality, without the risk of marginalization, pathologization, and violence.

4

HOMOSEXUALS AND ACCESS TO THE MINISTERIAL PRIESTHOOD

THE QUESTION AND ITS REPERCUSSION

The reception of homosexual persons in the Catholic Church also includes the question of their access to the ministerial priesthood. How should priests and candidates for the priesthood with this sexual orientation be treated? Initially, this matter is something internal to the Catholic Church. However, there are implications for the image of the homosexual person, with ethical and pastoral consequences. Therefore, people and institutions have manifested themselves with relevant contributions and reflections.

In 2018, the bishops of Italy had a meeting with the pope in which they dealt with the crisis of priestly and religious vocations, transparency and sobriety in the management of goods, and the merging of dioceses. After the pontiff's address, cameras were removed from the room, journalists left, doors closed, and a frank conversation began between him and the Italian episcopate. Then, the pope may have invited the bishops to a careful discernment of homosexual candidates for the priesthood, those who have these "deeply rooted" tendencies, and how the practice of "homosexual acts" can compromise seminary life, the young man himself, his future priesthood, and generate scandals. And he would have warned: "If you have the slightest doubt, it is better not to let them in." These probable statements of Francis can generate an image of homophobia and intolerance. However, it is necessary to understand them with respect to the Church's teaching in this regard, which has important nuances.

In this pontificate, the Roman Curia published a document on the priestly vocation. The gift of this vocation, given by God in the hearts of some people, is considered a requirement for the Church to offer them a serious path of formation. Vocations must be preserved and developed to produce ripe fruit. They are like a "diamond in the rough" that must be carved with skill, respect for people's consciences, and patience, so that they shine among God's people.[1] Candidates for the priesthood with a homosexual orientation were also considered, textually reiterating positions of an instruction published at the beginning of the pontificate of Benedict XVI, which states:

> The Church, while profoundly respecting the persons in question, cannot admit to the seminary or to holy orders those who practice homosexuality, present deep-seated homosexual tendencies or support the so-called "gay culture." Such persons, in fact, find themselves in a situation that gravely hinders them from relating correctly to men and women.... Different, however, would be the case in which one were dealing with homosexual tendencies that were only the expression of a transitory problem—for example, that of an adolescence not yet superseded. Nevertheless, such tendencies must be clearly overcome at least three years before ordination to the diaconate.[2]

This question also concerns the consecrated religious life, because all members of religious congregations, priests or not, men or women, have a vow of chastity in celibacy, and community life, and participate, according to the charism of their respective institute, in the evangelizing mission of the Church. To these, the orientation of ecclesiastical authority is "those who do not seem to be able to overcome their homosexual tendencies, or who maintain that it is possible to adopt a third way, 'living in an ambiguous state between celibacy and marriage' must be dismissed from the religious life."[3]

When they published the Roman instruction in the pontificate of Benedict XVI, the cardinal who signed the text stated in an interview that it was inappropriate to ordain homosexual candidates, even though there are priests of exemplary conduct with this sexual orientation.[4] Some who have the same opinion as the prefect praised the move. Others criticized it, thinking the Vatican wanted to fight sexual abuse scandals by punishing homosexuals. This is because there is an indirect association between homosexuality and pedophilia suggested in the document, where: "Norms concerning a specific question, made more urgent by the current situation, and that is: whether to admit to the seminary and to holy orders candidates who have deep-seated homosexual tendencies."[5] The reference to the current situation that makes the rules supposedly more urgent relates to the pedophilia scandals that were then widely reported. It was believed that the implementation of the instruction could solve or lessen the problem. But such scandals, critics argue, also have victims who are girls and women, and the admission of heterosexual people to the priesthood is not questioned.[6]

According to the instruction, it is up to the Church to define the requirements for ordination and to call those who are judged qualified. In the Latin rite, the commitment of celibacy is assumed; in the Eastern rites, either celibacy or a well-established (heterosexual) marriage. The candidate for the priesthood must reach the affective maturity that makes him capable of establishing a correct relationship with men and women. And with this maturity, he must develop spiritual fatherhood with the community entrusted to him. It is up to the bishop or religious superior to call the orders, after listening to those in charge of formation.[7]

The reception of the instruction, however, added new elements to the understanding of deeply rooted homosexual tendencies and gay culture. In the tradition of the Church, reception is how norms and doctrines are accepted and assimilated into the life of the local churches and become expressions of faith in them. It is a process by which, with the help of the Spirit's guidance, the people of God recognize intuitions or ideas and integrate them into the configuration and structure of their life and their worship, accepting a new witness to the truth and the forms of expression that correspond to it, because it is understood that they follow apostolic tradition. The process of reception is fundamental to the life and health of the Church as a pilgrim people in history for the fullness of the kingdom of God.[8] Local realities and different layers of interpretation play a very important role in this process, allowing for more nuanced and flexible understandings.

The then president of the German Episcopal Conference, Cardinal Karl Lehmann, stated that one should not understand deeply rooted homosexual tendencies as any same-sex tendencies, but those that are a serious obstacle to a correct relationship with men and women.[9] Following this interpretation, deeply rooted heterosexual tendencies are also a serious obstacle. The former Superior General of the Dominicans, Timothy Radcliffe, worked around the world with bishops and priests, diocesan and religious. He claimed that God no doubt calls homosexuals to the priesthood. And it states that they are among the most dedicated and impressive priests that he has found. Therefore, no priest who is convinced of his vocation should feel classified by the document as incapable. And it can be presumed that God will continue to call to the priesthood both homosexual and heterosexual men because He needs the gifts of both.

As for gay culture, Radcliffe says seminarians and priests should not attend gay bars and seminarians should not develop a gay subculture. Any sexual subculture, gay or straight, is incompatible with celibacy. But he questions whether supporting gay culture means just that. The instruction states that the Church must oppose unjust discrimination against homosexuals, just as it opposes racial discrimination (n. 2). This means, then, that all priests must be prepared to stand with the gays if they are oppressed. And be seen on their side.

Society, he continues, is obsessed with sex, and the Church should offer a model of healthy, non-compulsive acceptance of sexuality. The Catechism of the Council of Trent teaches that the priest must treat sex "preferably in moderation rather than in excess." There should be more attention to whom seminarians can hate than to whom they love. Racism, misogyny, and homophobia should indicate that someone may not be a model of Christ.[10]

The Conference of Swiss Bishops also spoke on this issue and admission to the priesthood:

> We are deeply grateful to all the priests who live their vocation with great fidelity. We are aware that in our priestly

> college and seminaries co-brothers live with heterosexual orientation and others with homosexual orientation. We respect each as a man and co-brother. We decide to live chastity regardless of our sexual orientation. Therefore, at the heart of our reflections on access to the priesthood, there is no question of sexual orientation, but the willingness to follow Christ consistently.[11]

As can be seen, the reception of the Roman instruction stimulated a creative fidelity in some segments of the Church. The reflection deepened, the concepts were nuanced and opened paths with a greater appreciation for the homosexual person.

In 2007, the Roman Curia released a new document with guidelines on the use of psychology in the admission and formation of candidates to the priesthood. Priesthood formation is understood as a configuration to Christ, the Good Shepherd. In this formation, we want to cultivate spiritual motivations and seek a human and affective balance, so that there is inner freedom in the relationship with the faithful. The use of psychology through testing and psychotherapy is recommended in certain circumstances but is not mandatory.

The training path must be interrupted if the candidate, despite his commitment and psychological support, is unable to "face realistically" his serious immaturity. Among them are mentioned: strong affective dependence, remarkable lack of freedom in relationships, excessive rigidity of character, lack of loyalty, uncertain sexual identity, and strongly rooted homosexual tendencies. The same is true in the case of excessive difficulty with celibacy, "lived as an obligation so painful as to compromise the emotional and relational balance."[12]

Note that homosexual orientation, although classified as serious immaturity, is not the cause of impediment to the priesthood, but the inability to deal with this orientation properly. The restriction of the previous document has been eased. And whoever the candidate is, he should not live celibacy at any price, sacrificing his emotional balance. This norm is known and very appropriate also for religious and lay faithful.

Amid all this controversy, however, the self-esteem of gay seminarians and priests is greatly bombarded. There needs to be an environment of trust where they can admit their condition, even if only for themselves and for their spiritual guides and their superiors. And may they talk, reflect, and pray about it. Otherwise, closeted homosexuality will have devastating effects on themselves and others. There is a lack of explicit models of homosexual holiness, known and esteemed in the Church, on which these people can be inspired.

DEEPENING THE ISSUE

Many dioceses and religious congregations are open to ordaining gay men committed to celibate life. They tend to be warm, intelligent, talented, and sensitive men, which are important qualities for ministry and religious life. Frequently, they stand out as liturgists and preachers, and exercise ministry creatively and efficiently. The vast majority keep their sexual orientation to themselves. Close friends and other homosexual priests know, but often parents and family members are not informed. Attentive parents and siblings may be suspicious, but in most cases do not touch on the subject.

Is it worth asking whether homosexuality is indeed a growing phenomenon in the priesthood or is there simply more visibility than in past generations? Maybe both of those things. It is quite likely that many of the homosexual priests of past generations had no idea of the nature of their sexuality. The last decades have seen a radical change in self-perception and awareness of homosexuals.[13] There are no precise statistics, but the proportion of homosexuals in the clergy is notorious to be much higher than in the rest of the population. And one cannot deny this presence also in female institutes.[14]

There were times when sexuality was treated as taboo. But even today many vocational groups, seminaries, houses of formation, parishes, communities, pastoral ministries, and movements do not speak clearly of this theme. Sometimes they mention it when related to others considered more important, such as celibacy and chastity. Other times sexuality is only spoken of negatively, as if it were itself a dangerous and sinful reality,[15] thus reliving a dualism that for many centuries has contaminated Christianity, despising the body, matter, and terrestrial life.

Even with taboo and dualism, historically there has been an influx of homosexuals into consecrated religious life and the priesthood. According to historian John Boswell, from the sixth to the thirteenth centuries, the Church provided these men and women with safe shelter during a chaotic and dangerous period. The consecrated celibate religious life offered women a way to escape the consequences of marriage, such as sleeping with a husband and having children, which could not only be undesirable but even life-threatening. Both sexes were given a means of avoiding conventional sexual roles. They could exercise power in religious communities, among other women, without being subordinated to the male head of the family.

Men could be part of a community of equals, in which all were men, without the responsibilities of parenthood or of running a home. They could exercise, through the priesthood, skills of care and service that, in other circumstances, were associated with women and were considered shameful to men. They could avoid war obligations and devote themselves to studying. Women could become literate and educated, a rare opportunity for their sex outside religious communities after the decline of the Roman Empire in the West. For Boswell, it is reasonable to believe that, in these circumstances, the priesthood and religious communities have exercised a particular attraction to homosexuals, especially in societies that treated them as strangers, and in which there was no other alternative to marriage conceived essentially as a heterosexual union. These people didn't even need spiritual motivation to join a same-sex community.[16]

This probably happened in most of the Church's history. Men and women of faith, with a homosexual orientation, naturally considered the consecrated religious life and the celibate priesthood attractive. It is no surprise that Catholic homosexuals, often profoundly spiritual people, with a desire to serve others and a natural inclination to the liturgical rite, are attracted to the priesthood and religious life. When entering the seminary, there is no longer a need to explain to family and friends why they do not have girlfriends and do not marry. The discipline of celibacy and the role of a Church spokesperson who establishes the discipline of clergy, are a powerful help to keep disturbing or even frightening sexual inclinations under control, at least for some.[17]

For the proper accompaniment of homosexual candidates to the priesthood and religious life, it is necessary that the institution—whether a diocese, parish, or institute—check if it is prepared for this type of vocation. They are people whose affection and sexuality go beyond the conventional, requiring different and specific treatment. It is an offense to the dignity of the human being to receive someone in an environment where people, especially those in charge of accompaniment, are not open to it. It is neither fair nor evangelical to introduce someone into an environment where they see them as abnormal, sick, or "poor thing." Nobody feels good about being mocked, seeing people whispering in corners, or hearing homophobic jokes. To receive a homosexual candidate, you need to create a welcoming environment, where the difference is not seen as a wound, sin, or something similar.[18]

These forms of hostility are not free. There are important indications that they are an unconscious fear of the human heart, refusing to reconcile with the truth itself. Psychologists find that one of the deepest fears is the fear of impotence and homosexuality as if it were a kind of castration.[19] As previously seen, the expression "so-and-so is not a man" or "so-and-so is not a woman" refers to the homosexual person, who witnesses this presumed castration. Therefore, without realizing it, a series of barriers are built against any supposed threat or contagious danger. Some gays and lesbians don't come out to themselves. Furthermore, the heterosexual person has a homosexual dimension in different proportions, according to the Kinsey scale.

When considering both factors—unconscious fear and a real major or minor component of homosexuality—it is explainable that one of the unconscious mechanisms of defense is aggression, contempt, and hostility toward the homosexual person. The fear of contagious danger, fanaticism, rigorism, and repugnance toward gays and lesbians reveals a need to hide the truth about themselves. Based on prejudices, there is often the fear of losing one's security in the face of what is different, strange, and unknown, cataloging it as dangerous and inferior. The greater the fanaticism and repugnance against homosexuality, the greater the need to conceal one's existence, or a complete refusal to reconcile oneself with one's truth.[20]

Pope Francis warns against the rigid, against this kind of fanaticism and repugnance. "Hypocrites," he points out, is a word that Jesus often addresses to rigid people, because "behind the rigidity there is always something hidden, in many cases a double life." In fact, "rigidity is not a gift from God; meekness, goodness, benevolence, forgiveness, yes; but rigidity, no!" There is also something unhealthy. How hard people suffer. When they are sincere and realize this, they suffer because they cannot have the freedom of the children of God, they do not know how to walk in the law of the Lord and are not blessed.[21] The rigid people with double lives show themselves as beautiful and honest, but they do bad things when no one sees them. Certainly, there are those who "use rigidness to cover weaknesses, sins, personality flaws, and they use rigidness to rank themselves above others."[22]

In seminaries and houses of formation, even when they are welcomed, homosexual candidates may live with considerable fear that their sexual orientation will become an obstacle on their way to ordination. In some environments, they must deal with the implications of being part of a minority. Their spiritual and emotional needs require sensible counsel and guidance from spiritual advisors and seminary faculty. But on the other hand, homosexual seminarians and priests feel the need for friendship with other homosexuals. This can lead to a social life consisting essentially of other men with a homosexual orientation, creating a gay subculture in dioceses and seminaries. Consequently, heterosexual men in environments with a significant number of homosexuals may experience a sense of destabilization, with a certain insecurity and the impression that they do not fit there. On both the psychic and spiritual levels, they are not comfortable. Seminary instructors need to be aware of this phenomenon.[23]

Regarding the observance of chastity, a commandment for every single or married Christian, one should consider what first defines it, that is, the integration of sexuality in the person, in their unity of body and soul.[24] This integration is a gradual path and can only be successful if the person lives in peace with their sexuality, being able to relate and love their neighbor and themself, within their life choice. The conducts and paths in this field are important but must never dispense this integration under penalty of nullifying the person at a human and affective level. Recognizing and assuming one's sexual orientation is necessary to integrate it well. The opposite of this is closeted sexual orientation.

About this, the Dominican Donald Goergen states:

> Religious communities do not benefit from closeted homosexuality. I do not mean that men need to make public their sexuality, a notion that seems to be a strange curse of our period of history. By closeted homosexuals, I mean closeted men about themselves. That is, they are significantly out of touch with their sexuality and thus are unable to accept the degree or type of homosexuality present in them; as a

> result, they are men who live in denial, fear, and hatred of themselves. For homosexual men to live in religious communities, they need to be comfortable enough not to fear their homosexuality, and they certainly need to be able to recognize who they are in front of trusted friends.[25]

Such a risk persists. For many young people today, celibate life presents itself as a good opportunity not to face personal situations related to affection and sexuality. However, the choice of celibacy only postpones the problems. Sooner or later, they return with much more force and without control, because they have been "swept under the carpet." Seriously concerning, therefore, is the behavior of those who want to solve problems of affection and sexual order with pious advice appealing to Jesus, making it a kind of "cosmic carpet" under which very serious situations are thrown in the desperate search for magical solutions that don't exist.

The irruption of problems is more explosive and irrational if they have been accompanied by a pedagogy of repression. When feelings are repressed for too long, they end up erupting drastically, without control and the conscious will of the individual. There are those who, consciously or unconsciously, hide their condition under the guise of orthodoxy, fidelity, rigorism, moralism, and ecclesiastical looks. Some, to disguise their situation, cultivate exaggerated forms of piety and spiritualism. In the end, they are "unresolved" people who, in the bitterness of tumultuous sexuality, end up hindering the lives of others and the dynamics of evangelization. In place of the pedagogy of repression, there must be a sexual education capable of guiding one's conscience, seeking a realization consistent with their sexuality.[26]

Some homosexual priests follow the social instinct of finding the company of similar individuals, priests or not, sharing their identity with trusted friends. Thus, they form gay networks or subcultures. But some of them use it to cover up their sexual activity, believing that the only responsibility to the Church is a certain discretion. Religious and diocesan leaders need to distinguish between the celibate, homosexual, or heterosexual, who struggles and sometimes fails to be chaste; and the priest or religious person who coldly exploits the priesthood or institute for its destructive purposes.[27]

THE PEDOPHILIA SCANDALS AND HOMOSEXUALITY

The Catholic Church has been hard-hit by scandals of sexual abuse of minors committed by priests. These came to the surface with more intensity in the last two decades, in unprecedented waves of denunciation that had wide coverage in the media. In some countries, the effects were quite devastating. It is appropriate to reflect on what can be learned from this tragedy, as well as to avoid creating scapegoats, and mistakenly blaming and penalizing people for that evil. Frequently homosexuals are suspected of being pedophiles because the term homosexual has historically emerged to replace the pejorative pederast, which etymologically means men who have erotic relationships with boys.

The reported cases occurred in the last seventy years. However old they are, they left deep and painful wounds in the lives of the victims. In these crimes, the Church authorities did not report cases of abuse to the civilian power. They often preferred agreement with the victims and their families, through indemnity, and the removal of the accused priests, who said they were sorry and were referred to psychological treatment. Many of these priests, transferred to other places, repeated countless times until everything was denounced with great indignation and pain.

You can see there is a residue of Christendom, the times of the Christian confessional state. The problem used to be solved within the Church, which must proceed as a family. At most, the ecclesiastical tribunal was used to try crimes committed by clerics. However, the question did not cross the ecclesial border. This procedure that lasted until the end of the twentieth century is, in essence, a refusal to adapt to modernity, a refusal to accept impersonal and equal law for all. A psychologist's opinion presented to the North American bishops in 1992 also contributed to this. It was believed that pedophilia could be cured and that the priests involved should be given a chance.

Since the pontificate of Benedict XVI, there have been important changes in the Church in confronting these crimes. The procedures in cases of denunciation have been unified and provide for referral to the Roman Curia. Civil law should always be followed relating to reporting the crime to the competent authority. During the preliminary reporting phase and until the case is completed, the local bishop may impose preventive measures to protect the community and victims, restricting the activities of any priest in his diocese. Benedict XVI and Francis met the victims and asked forgiveness from God and them for the faults committed, expressing appreciation for their reports and sensitivity to their pain. Several bishops asked for resignation for recognizing their omission in the face of crimes committed by their priests.

Francis summoned all the presidents of national episcopal conferences to a meeting in the Vatican to address the protection of minors in the Catholic Church. Extensive reports, research, and expert opinions served as a subsidy. The pope recognizes that sexual abuse of minors was taboo in the past when it was known of its existence, but no one spoke of it. What happens in the Church is connected to what happens in society. Even today, the available statistics compiled by various national and international organizations—WHO, UNICEF, Interpol, Europol, and others—do not show the true extent of the phenomenon that is underestimated because many cases of sexual abuse of minors are not reported, especially the many committed within the family. Added to this is the scourge of sex tourism. According to data from the World Tourism Organization, in 2017, three million people worldwide traveled to have sex with minors. Such abuses are always the consequence of abuse of power, in which the position of the inferiority of the helpless abused is explored, and their conscience and their psychological and physical fragility are manipulated.

In the case of priests, Francis associates this evil with clericalism, an anomaly in the way of understanding authority in the Church, common in many communities where sexual abuse, power, and conscience occurred. Clericalism, favored by both priests and laity, helps to perpetuate many of the evils denounced today. It is necessary to deal decisively with the abuse of minors, inside and outside the Church, to proclaim the Gospel to the little ones, and to protect them from the ravenous wolves. No abuse should ever be covered up. Whatever is done to eradicate the "culture of abuse" in Catholic communities will only result in a healthy and realistic transformation with the active participation of all Church members.[28]

Clericalism is an evil that Pope Francis often denounces with courage. A face of this evil is precisely the presumption of impunity on the part of priests who sexually abuse minors. Clericalism comes not only from the clergy but also from the laity whenever they do not react properly. There are cases of parents of abused children and young people who refused to report, or even severely punished their children who did. Unfortunately, there is a culture of abuse, which silences not only pedophilia by clergy but also pedophilia by family fathers and violence against women by their husbands or partners.

The pedophilia scandal has brought further developments. Not many have tried to blame homosexuality for the abuses of the clergy, especially in the contemporary culture they consider permissive. Others have tried to blame priestly celibacy, which they consider a hallucinatory denial of sexuality and a fearful thing. As has been said, most cases occur within the family, indoors, and the responsible person is often the victim's father or stepfather. The offender is not celibate and has a heterosexual married life. When these cases are reported, common sense does not blame marriage or heterosexuality for the offense. But if the person is celibate, they often blame celibacy; and if he is homosexual, they blame homosexuality.

It should be noted that the main reports on the sexual abuse of minors by the clergy, made with a broad scientific basis by the U.S., German, and Australian governments, do not associate this crime with homosexuality or celibacy. These associations are due to certain types of prejudice: homophobia and celibacy. Scapegoats are created for mistaken reasons. The presence of homosexuals in the clergy, as well as priestly celibacy, should not be taboo subjects, but discussing them in the context of sexual abuse is a rather harmful mistake.

It can be said that the Church is learning hard to deal with this issue. In places where more cases of abuse have appeared and appropriate measures have been taken, there has been a drastic reduction in new cases. May the conscience of the errors committed in scandals lead, with the grace of God, to proclaim the Gospel to the little ones and to protect them from the ravenous wolves.

EMERGING PATHS

Something very relevant about the access of homosexual candidates to the priesthood is the existence, although very exceptional, of openly gay priests. They present reports about their reality that had wide dissemination and caused reflection. There are two important examples in the United States: Fred Daley and Gregory Greiten.

Fred Daley is a parish priest in Syracuse, New York. When he began to admit to himself his attraction to people of the same sex, he experienced a great inner torment. With the help of advice and spiritual guidance, he began to accept himself and love himself as a gay man. In 2002, the sexual abuse scandal erupted in the United States, and several Catholic church leaders began blaming gay priests for the crisis. Daley faced a dilemma: "I knew that was not true. I concluded that if I should live with integrity and preach the gospel without dishonorable concessions, I needed to come out of the closet publicly." The decision was preceded by prayer and strengthened by consultations with his spiritual advisor and auxiliary bishop.

The public revelation took place at the liturgical feast of the Annunciation. Daley realized that people facing personal conflicts perceived him as more approachable because they knew he also had personal conflicts. Any illusion of being on a clerical pedestal happily fell apart. And confirms what Father Henri Nouwen said: "We tend to be compassionate as we suffer the Passion in our own lives."[29]

Gregory Greiten, in turn, is a priest in Milwaukee, Wisconsin. He lived a long and painful process until he accepted himself as gay. He then made his sexual orientation public, with the approval of his bishop. Greiten strongly criticizes the silence that the Church ends up imposing on religious and gay priests as if they did not exist. There are no authentic models of healthy, balanced, gay, and celibate priests who set an example for young and old people who are struggling to accept their sexual orientation. This only perpetuates toxic shame and systemic secrecy.

Therefore, he committed:

> I will not be silent any longer; the price to pay is way too great. I must speak my truth. I have lived far too many years chained up and imprisoned in the closet behind walls of shame, trauma and abuse because of the homophobia and discrimination so prevalent in my church and the world. But rather, today, I chart a new course in freedom and in integrity knowing that there is nothing that anyone can do to hurt or destroy my spirit any longer. First steps in accepting and loving the person God created me to be.[30]

As a priest of the Catholic Church, Greiten asks forgiveness from his LGBTQ+ brothers and sisters for remaining silent in the face of actions and omissions from his community of faith toward LGBTQ+ Catholics and non-Catholics. He commits to no longer living in the shadows of the secret, to be authentically gay, and to embrace the person God created him to be. In his life and priestly ministry, he asserts: "I, too, will help you, whether you are gay or straight, bisexual or transgender, to be your authentic self—to be fully alive living in your image and likeness of God. In reflecting our God-images out into the world, our world will be a brighter, more tolerant place." And he recalls Saint Catherine of Siena, doctor of the Church: "Be who God meant you to be and you will set the world on fire."[31]

In both cases, this does not refer to the supposed curse of the present time to make public one's sexual orientation, but it refers to the reasons that deserve to be considered. There is homophobia and transphobia in society and the Church that need to be properly addressed. There are still many environments in which gays and lesbians do not come out publicly. In politics, for example, heads of state are rare. In Brazil, so far there have been no openly homosexual presidents of the republic, state governors, or mayors of capitals. In the clergy and consecrated religious life, this is almost unthinkable. Fathers Daley and Greiten chart a lonely and heroic path. They are at a frontier of risk, but also of opportunity for building a better world, where people can live and breathe in their gender and sexuality, without the risk of marginalization, pathologization, and violence.

In the pope's address to the Italian bishops, in which he talked about homosexual candidates for the priesthood, he said that the Church should be a mother and said this prayer: "May Mary, our Mother, help us so that the Church may be a mother."[32] The Church must be helped in this noble and loving mission. The children of the Church have an undeniable potential to be offered, which must never be wasted. But they can also have wounds and demand care that must not be neglected. Only in this way can the maternal mission of the Church succeed.

The gift of the priestly vocation, granted by God also in the hearts of some homosexual men, demands the Church's maturity and breadth of horizons to know how to welcome and propose the right path of formation. Only in this way can these vocations be preserved and developed to produce ripe fruit. The same goes for homosexual women and men in consecrated religious life. They are also like a diamond in the rough to be carved with skill, respect for people's consciences, and patience so that they shine amid God's people. One cannot despise these divine gifts by burying a treasure, as does the evil and lazy servant of the Parable of the Talents (Matt 25:14–30).

On the path of formation, an environment of trust is necessary where everyone can recognize and accept their condition in peace, without misunderstanding, fear, or hatred of themselves. Let them do so in their conscience before God, sharing with their spiritual guides and trustworthy people. Study, reflection, prayer, and open dialogue are needed, so that they can continue with proper self-esteem and determination in the ways of the Lord. May the Church not lose talents and not fail to produce mature fruit.

5

NEW PERSPECTIVES, THEOLOGICAL AND PASTORAL CHALLENGES

HOMOSEXUAL UNIONS AND THE ECCLESIAL DEBATE

In the preparation for the synod on the family, other ecclesial voices manifested themselves besides Rome, when some answers to the preparatory questionnaires were made public. Regarding homosexuality, the German and Swiss dioceses responded critically. Based on the humanities and medicine, the German faithful stated that sexual orientation is an unalterable disposition and not chosen by the individual. Therefore, talking about "homosexual tendency" caused irritation and was perceived as a discriminatory expression.[1] In Switzerland, most of the faithful consider it to be just the desire of homosexuals to have relationships and form unions. The demand that they live in sexual abstinence is rejected as unjust and inhumane. It is unacceptable for homosexuals to be regarded only as recipients of pastoral care, seen as sick people or in need of help. They are to be treated with respect and their participation should be appreciated in the Church. The discourse on the impossibility of any kind of analogy between (heterosexual) marriage and the homosexual union is not accepted. The Church is to recognize, cherish, and bless homosexual unions, helping the members of these unions to live important values that have, indeed, an analogy to marriage.[2]

The theologian Juan Masiá Clavel, a Spanish Jesuit living in Japan and a bioethics researcher, also made his answer public. For him, it is necessary to promote the welcome of homosexual persons and unions, as well as families thus constituted, in the daily and sacramental life of ecclesial communities without discrimination. Civil legislation on homosexual unions should be respectfully recognized. A revision of biblical, moral, and theological hermeneutics regarding sexuality in the light of the human sciences is necessary, especially pluriform sexuality and the educational requirements for inclusive coexistence. The impossibility of analogy, even remote, between homosexual unions and God's plan for marriage cannot be affirmed as the teaching of the Church. It would be presumptuous to possess the right and definitive knowledge of this supposed divine design.

Masiá asserts that both the Second Vatican Council's definition of a spousal union as an "intimate community of life and love" (GS 48), and the biblical image of people who leave their respective families and go out of themselves so that two become one, remaining together along a path of love and life (cf. Gen 2:24), can lend themselves to a homosexual spousal union. Openness to life does not exist only in generating a new life as a couple formed by man and woman, but also when a homosexual couple legally and responsibly resorts to assisted procreation, the adoption of a life already born, or when dedicated in various ways to contribute as a family to the social promotion of life. The possible objections in each case against an adoption, or the use of medically assisted procreation, should be the same as in a similar case of a heterosexual couple. Theological moral reflection on sexuality must be reviewed considering that sexual orientation is not a choice, nor can it be said that its exercise is moral or immoral. It will be moral or immoral for the same reasons as heterosexual relationships. The same ethical questions should apply to both: if the relationship is reasonable, responsible, and honest with oneself and with the other person, if it is loving, humanizing, and helps fair personal growth.[3]

Untying the knots of literalism and fundamentalism that bind the biblical reading is necessary, Masiá observes, favoring a hermeneutic that makes possible a critical and Christian interpretation of the Bible. It is necessary to break the knots of prejudice that bind pastoral care and the commandment to love, thus freeing mercy, compassion, and tenderness. Certain questions should be focused more on the ethics of relationships than ethics of sexuality, as a plurality of models of relationship and family, rather than a single thought presumed to know the divine design. They should be focused on the ethics of evangelical values in the situation, instead of abstract disembodied norms.[4]

Given the results of the synod on the family, including the post-synodal exhortation, theologians Todd Salzman and Michael Lawler address those who support same-sex marriage as a way of living with dignity, believing that the denial of this right is unjust discrimination. There is still hope in *Amoris Laetitia* for the realization of these aspirations. This hope lies in the theme of graduality that permeates the document. As the number of Catholic faithful at ease with same-sex marriage grows, something that is already demonstrated by world statistics, it will gradually become accepted as communion in certain circumstances for divorced and remarried people, without an annulment of the previous union. The challenge for gays and lesbians is to demonstrate that their marriages are as fulfilling as heterosexual marriages from a human and Christian perspective. Catholic doctrine on the authority and inviolability of personal conscience, reiterated by Francis, naturally applies to the decision of gay and lesbian Catholics to marry as much as it applies to any other moral decision.[5] If the strength of the family lies essentially in their ability to love and teach to love (AL 53), it is up to them to demonstrate how their unions fulfill this function.

Regarding pastoral care, there are different practices. For decades in the Netherlands, according to a survey by the University of Utrecht, 80 percent of Catholic clergy celebrate same-sex unions, even without formal ecclesiastical approval. And half the clergy celebrate these unions within Catholic temples.[6] The wide acceptance of homosexuality in Dutch society, which includes a remarkable pastoral openness of the Catholic Church at the local level in this matter, contributes to this. In Germany, the issue is currently being discussed. The president of the German Episcopal Conference, Cardinal Reinhard Marx, affirms that homosexual partners can receive the blessing "in the sense of pastoral accompaniment" in the Catholic Church. But no marriage-like relationship can be blessed. This is similar to what the Swiss bishops defend, as noted earlier.

There is also an intermediate position defended by Juan Masiá based on suggestions sent by Japanese Catholics to the synod of bishops on the family. While the Church institution does not take steps to change or abolish canonical determinations, churches-faith-communities could and should take effective and positive steps in welcoming people. The practice of the Catholic Church in Japan, approved by Rome, celebrating in the Catholic temple a religious ceremony for the union of non-baptized and nonbelievers, can serve as an example. This has been done there for many decades. In the popular expression there, they say, "They marry in the Church, but not by the Church," to refer to the religious celebration without canonical validity. A Catholic rite is celebrated for the union of people who contracted the marriage civilly. This could also serve remarried Catholics and nonheterosexual couples.

For Masiá, those who rightly insist on doing everything possible to defend, protect, and promote the institution of marriage and the family can be reassured. This is because a same-sex union does not threaten but supports the marriage institution by insisting on the social formalization of the bond, rather than reducing it to the private sphere of an actual coexistence with uncertain stability. There are indications that a culture of provisionality increases divorce, as well as a lack of interest in civilly formalizing unions. Precisely for this reason, there is the interest, desire, and demand of LGBTQ+ couples for the social, juridical, and cultural recognition of their marriage union that could and should also be religious recognition.[7]

The homosexual union does not compete with the heterosexual union. In a heterosexual union, even if celebrated with the rite of marriage, if one of the spouses is homosexual, complementarity between man and woman is not given. The sacrament of marriage in these circumstances is invalid, according to ecclesiastical law (cf. CCL, 1983, can 1095, n. 3). Unfortunately, due to the homophobia still present in certain social media, many gays and lesbians are under pressure to contract heterosexual unions. It's the way they find to escape prejudice. This has been happening for centuries and brings much suffering to the people involved. It is necessary to put an end to this situation. The faithful need to know that a heterosexual union is not a solution for a homosexual person.

Incidentally, in the biblical account of creation, there is a very important aspect about the complementarity between man and woman. The Lord, in creating the human being and not wanting them to be alone, also made a corresponding helper who was presented to the man. And the man exclaimed: "This at last is bone of my bones / and flesh of my flesh; / this one shall be called Woman [literally human], / for out of Man this one was taken" (Gen 2:23). It is the man who recognizes and appreciates the help that corresponds to him and names her. It is not the Lord who imposes it on man. From this recognition and appreciation, the first conjugal union begins. However, the recognition of the human being about their complementarity is fundamental to the conjugal union. Hence the free consent of the spouses without which their union is invalid. This is as important at the beginning of creation as it is today.

GENDER AND SEXUAL ORIENTATION IN DEBATE

The reality of LGBTQ+ people, their conflicts, and their sufferings is often absent in official Catholic Church statements. In the Latin American context, for example, the Aparecida document dealing with the poor, the excluded, and those who suffer, makes a broad list: "migrants, victims of violence, displaced people and refugees, victims of human trafficking and kidnappings, the disappeared, people sick with HIV and endemic diseases, drug addicts, adults, boys and girls who are victims of prostitution, pornography and violence or of child labor, abused women, victims of exclusion and traffic for sexual exploitation, differently-abled people, large groups of unemployed men and women, those excluded by technological illiteracy, street people in large cities, the indigenous and Afro-Americans, landless peasants and miners."[8] Unfortunately, LGBTQ+ stayed out. In many ecclesial settings, it is very uncomfortable to talk about them. It is common in the suffering of this population to be ignored or silenced.

Other times the theme appears in the context of shallow controversy and repudiation when some seek to fight the supposed gender ideology. There are publications in the Catholic milieu with great diffusion, some even caricaturing issues of gender and sexual orientation. This is the case of the teaching material in several languages distributed at World Youth Day in 2013 in Rio de Janeiro. This one features a drawing of a sitting man wondering: "What gender will I choose for this year?" On another page, the drawing of a naked boy looking at his penis, wondering: "Am I not a man? Me? So…what is this?"[9] Obviously, no one chooses to be gay or lesbian as they choose where to travel on vacation. No transgender—a boy or girl—is surprised by their anatomy simply by hearing third parties call it a mistake. This is gloating about the drama experienced by so many people. Such caricatures are unfair and cruel. They are examples of homophobic and transphobic bullying, fought today even by sensible Catholic manuals.

There are also publications from representative Catholic institutions that cite the work of Judith Butler as the main source of gender ideology, for proposing a "variable construction of identity." One of the most contested statements of this author is that there is no gender identity behind gender expressions and that such identity is performatively constituted through expressions taken as its results. At this point, it is based on Nietzsche's assumption that there is no being behind doing, realizing, and becoming. The doer is a mere fiction added to the work. This is everything. For her, gender is an anti-substantialism concept with which one intends to defeat the metaphysics of identity.[10] In fact, in her work, there is an anti-metaphysical perspective. But in linking Butler to gender ideology, the following accusations made to this ideology also fall on her: wanting to deny the body as a legitimate expression of the individual's identity, as capable of expressing such identity appropriately; wanting to eliminate all differences and all social structures; and wanting to demolish the primary foundation of society constituted by the family.[11]

Her book *Gender Trouble* (2008) received strong criticism, such as the alleged denial of the natural difference between the sexes. Her lectures in Brazil were the target of hostile public protests. In the face of criticism, Butler explained her motivations. She recognizes the complexity of gender, involving nature, culture, and the individual, but without definite, irreconcilable positions with Christian-inspired anthropology:

> There are hormonal and physiological differences in chromosomes between men and women. But although we work with binary thinking there are variations, a continuum between one and the other. Research reveals that biology is not determining, that gender results from a unique combination, in each of us, of biological, sexual, social function, self-understanding, and gender representation. It has been

found that hormones are interactive and there are several ways in which they can be activated. Even the development of neurons is linked to the environment. What happens partially depends on the life you live.[12]

Butler's thought does not reject innate elements that permeate the reality of gender in people and the perception of oneself, but is very careful to capture the specificity of those who for some reason do not fit into the binary model:

> One can debate which aspects of gender are innate or acquired, but it is more important to recognize the involuntary effect of gender designation and the deeply consolidated resistance [of some] to such designation.…I accept that some people have a deep sense of their gender and that this should be respected. I can't explain this deep feeling, but it exists for many. It may be a limitation to my analysis I personally don't have that deep sense of gender. It may be that this absence is what motivated my theory.[13]

It does not delegitimize cisgender and heterosexual people, but urges that others are not delegitimized or harassed:

> Some people live in peace with the gender assigned to them, but others suffer when they are forced to conform to social norms that nullify the deeper sense of who they are and who they wish to be. For these people, it is an urgent need to create the conditions for a life possible to live.[…]In fact, something that concerns me is how often people who do not fit into gender norms and heterosexual expectations are harassed, assaulted, and murdered.…
>
> Did the book deny the existence of a natural difference between the sexes? In no way, although it highlights the existence of divergent scientific paradigms to determine the differences between the sexes, and it notes that some bodies have mixed attributes that hinder their classification. I have also stated that human sexuality takes different forms and that we should not assume that knowing a person's gender gives us any clue about their sexual orientation.[14]

The author follows the purpose of finding a better vocabulary for ways of living with gender and sexuality that do not fit so easily into the binary norm. She searches for the word in which the existing complexity can be recognized, where the fear of marginalization, pathologization, and violence is radically eliminated. And she glimpses something more important than producing new gender formulations, which is to build a world in which people can live and breathe within their own sexuality and their own gender.[15] Her thinking is under construction. At one point she turned to Nietzsche and an anti-metaphysical perspective, but that does not sum up her thought. Excerpts from Butler are frequently quoted to make a reductionist cut of her work.

To simply identify this author with gender ideology is to disqualify it unduly because ideology is an idea that takes over people's thinking uncritically. This is moral panic. Such panic is characterized by a disproportionate collective reaction of fear in the face of demands for social change, faced with a supposed threat perceived as something that puts at risk a crucial component of society, which is the social order itself. On the contrary, it is necessary to discern the elements of current gender and sexual orientation studies that contribute to the advancement of these issues in the theological and pastoral field. The good missionary recognizes the work of the Holy Spirit in the heart of human beings and cultures, even in non-Christian civilizations and religions. They know that the Spirit manifests in the Church and its members, but also that the Spirit's presence and action are universal, without limits of space and time. The Spirit cares for and germinates "'seeds of the Word,' to be found in human initiatives—including religious ones—and in mankind's efforts to attain truth, goodness and God himself" (RM 28).[16] The same goes for gender studies and the pursuit of the good of the LGBTQ+ population.

In the Christian theological horizon, some reflections contemplate contemporary perspectives. Giannino Piana proposes not to renounce the difference between man and woman and its fundamental importance, which is rooted in anatomical sex and constitutes the archetype from which humanity originates. Social and cultural processes should be made evident without entirely ignoring the biological component, the genetic and neuronal structure of the human subject. The role of culture and social structures should be considered, recognizing the merit of gender studies in capturing the relevance of personal experiences in defining gender identity. This contributes to overcoming prejudices that cause severe discrimination, which led to and still lead to the marginalization of LGBTQ+.

The position of the Catholic Church, according to Piana, has been characterized by a radical defense of biological data, inserting it in the order of creation. The Church has frequently regarded criticism of this as an attack on divine sovereignty. One aspect of truth cannot be denied in this position: the commitment to defend the basis of the human being that would be seriously compromised by the total deconstruction of biological identity. But this should not lead to the refusal of reflection on human nature and natural law, even if it has long assumed rigidly physical-biological connotations. The history of Christian thought brings valuable contributions.

Thomas Aquinas, a scholastic theologian, states clearly that the concepts of nature and natural law are only applied to humans analogically. This has a double nature: as an animal, which is common to other animals; and as a man, which is proper to man, to the extent that reason distinguishes the vile from the honest. Such nature is *natura ut ratio* (nature as reason), reason being the qualifying trait.[17] Today we would say culture. This introduces the possibility of intervention in natural dynamics. Thus, a vision of patristic thought inherited from Platonic dualism and Stoic naturalism was overcome, which introduced into Christian morality an absolutist and static position. Scholasticism introduced attention to the cultural factor, to the dynamic and evolutionary aspect.

Gender studies, concludes Piana, are a significant provocation to become aware of the human's worth, to think about identity from a greater awareness of oneself and one's freedom, considering the importance of subjective decisions and personal lifestyles. This avoids forms of flattening reality around universalist paradigms, which do not respect individual diversities. Ethics, including its aspect of Christian inspiration, must be attentive to this new interpretation of the human world and ground its orientations on broader bases, considering the complex dynamics that govern the construction of behaviors, linked to structural and cultural processes of the society in which one is immersed.[18]

Coping with LGBT violence and discrimination has led the state of Brazil to take important measures. These measures inevitably focus on the debate about gender and sexual orientation. In Brazil, the federal government has determined that police reports include the items "sexual orientation," "gender identity," and "social name." Social name is understood as the name by which transvestites and transsexuals identify themselves and are identified by society. The reason presented is the need to give visibility to violent crimes against the LGBT population,[19] and thus favors actions and public policies to face them.

The Ministry of Education (MEC) established that in the preparation and implementation of curriculum proposals and pedagogical projects, education systems and basic education schools should ensure guidelines and practices with the aim of "combating any forms of discrimination based on sexual orientation and gender identity" of students, teachers, managers, employees, and their families. The objective is to prevent school dropouts, resulting from cases of discrimination, harassment, and violence in schools, because this evasion is a serious attack on the right to education.[20] Added to this is the decision of the Supreme Federal Court (STF) to criminalize homophobic and transphobic conduct, which involves hateful aversion to the sexual orientation or gender identity of someone, framing them in the Racism Law (STF, 2019).

When the end to discrimination based on gender identity and sexual orientation was proposed at the U.N., as seen before (ch. 3), the Holy See expressed its opposition. Recalling the healthy secularity of the state, the Holy See claimed that this could become an instrument of pressure against those who consider homosexual behavior morally unacceptable, do not recognize the homosexual union as a family, nor its equivalence to the heterosexual union, nor their right to adoption and assisted reproduction.

As for the scope and implications of this legislation on sexual orientation and gender identity, it is worth asking: Is the accusation of gender ideology relevant? The resolution on police reports wants to give visibility to certain crimes to better face them. The Resolution CNE/CP 1/2018 aims to prevent bullying and school dropouts. The STF decision clarifies in the sentence itself that "it does not reach or restrict or limit the exercise of religious freedom." The faithful and ministers have the right to preach and disseminate, as well as to teach according to their doctrinal or theological orientation, "as long as such manifestations do not constitute hate speech, understood exteriorizations that incite discrimination, hostility or violence against people because of their sexual orientation or gender identity" (STF, 2019). Therefore, in the horizon of the healthy secularism of the state, such legislation is not an instrument of pressure against the right of churches or religious confessions to peacefully teach about sexuality, marriage, and family, but it is a way of defending vulnerable people who are frequently humiliated, harassed and even massacred. Thus, it does not fit here the accusation of gender ideology.

To broaden the reflection, it is appropriate to question whether the alert of the synod on this ideology, endorsed by Pope Francis (AL 56), applies or not to the LGBTQ+ citizenship and gender studies exposed above. First, the difference and natural reciprocity between men and women do not apply to homosexual persons. Encouraging or embarrassing gays and lesbians to enter a union with another sex does not perform the sacrament of marriage, but it nulls unions. Second, the personal identity and affective intimacy of LGBTQ+ in their relationships are not radically detached from the biological diversity between man and woman, but deeply linked to this diversity that is much more complex. Biologically, there are not only cisgender and heterosexual people but also transgender, homosexual, and bisexual, although this reality is not only biological. Third, recognizing LGBTQ+ is never an option, nor is it individualistic; rather the truth that imposes itself in the lives of many people often contradicting harshly what they and their families would want for themselves. Fourth, it is not a matter of separating biological sex and sociocultural function from gender, but a matter of considering the role of the brain in the biology of sex, without reducing it simply to anatomy and genitalia.

ADULT CHRISTIANITY AND BROADENING HORIZONS

To those who believe in God the Creator and his creative reason, the world can be presented as the book of one and indivisible nature, as Benedict XVI says, in which nothing is outside this reason (see ch. 1). If by analogy to the Book of Revelation (the Bible as a whole), the world resembles a book to be read and understood, one can explore this metaphor. The Bible contains dozens of books, employs more than one language, and uses various literary genres. It was written by dozens of different authors over a millennium. Biblical studies over the centuries are vast and endless. The Book of Nature, in turn, also has its multiplicity and complexity, its languages and literary genres. Its reading and interpretation are still in process. Gender and sexual-orientation issues are part of this multiplicity and complexity.

The correct reading of the language of creation requires the care indicated regarding the natural law. It is necessary to avoid a resigned submission to the physical and biological laws of nature considering human freedom, culture, and its evolution. The unbearable heteronomy must be avoided, with data imposed from the outside on the consciousness of the subject, independent of reason itself and subjectivity. It is also necessary to avoid the undue naturalization of anthropological positions, which are historical and conditioned, such as slavery and the prohibition of interest.[21] Once the historical rooting of morality is recognized, rejecting a fixist morality, it is appropriate to reconsider some judgments about gender studies and to open the way for other reflections. This path is encouraged by the challenges launched by Francis to go to the existential peripheries, question outdated ecclesial structures, reread the Gospel in the light of contemporary culture, take on conflicts, and heal wounds.

As he well observed, Jesus did not present Himself as an enemy of the pleasurable things of life and was far from the philosophies that despised the body, matter, and realities of this world. However, these dualisms have had a remarkable influence on some Christian thinkers throughout history to the point of disfiguring the Gospel (LS 98). Such contempt, coupled with a certain enmity toward pleasure, fueled a strongly prohibitive morality. Benedict XVI recognized this prohibition. He stated that Christianity is not a set of prohibitions, but a positive option. And he added that it is very important to highlight this again because this consciousness today has almost completely disappeared.[22] It is very good that a pope has recognized this, for in Christianity there is a centuries-old tradition of insistence on prohibition, sin, guilt, condemnation, and fear. Historiography speaks of a "pastoral of fear" that vehemently blames people and threatens them with eternal damnation to obtain their conversion.[23]

This is not restricted to the past. Even today, in various churches and Christian environments, many interpret the doctrine in an extremely restrictive and condemnatory way, with an obsession with sin, especially regarding sex. Prohibitions linked to the Christian message often have more repercussions within and outside the Church than their positive content. There is an excessive focus on prohibition.

It is essential to seek in the Christian message its positive component, including the scope of sexuality, so that this message may be good news (gospel). Only in this way can one live the freedom of God's children, experiencing the light yoke and soft burden offered by Jesus.

We are living in a time of accelerated changes in society that, in turn, are linked to paradigm changes. In some subjects, many believers face disagreement between their conscience and the position of the Church. Theologian Karl Rahner developed a concept that can help in this impasse: that of a "mature Christian."[24] This expression already existed and circulated widely in Rahner's time. It corresponds to an authentic task of Christians and at the same time can mean a threat to ecclesial reality. The situation today and that one must face as an adult, has peculiarities. Unlike in the past, it is now more difficult to formulate clear and general rules about what should be done. Naturally, there are still norms in moral and social life that must be respected, but the field and the sense of what cannot be regulated in a univocal way through general norms have greatly increased. The scope of what cannot be determined only with these norms has grown, whether in society, politics, cultural life, or the configuration of personal life.

Maturity is courage and determination to make responsible decisions that cannot be legitimized by general and widely known norms. Wisdom, discernment, a supernatural moral instinct, and docility to the Holy Spirit belong to maturity. This, in turn, presupposes openness of mind, liberation from all fanaticism, willingness to learn, mastery of one's aggressiveness, and patience.

Theologically, today a Christian who is educated and lucid is always found in need of reflecting on the Church's message and faith, relating them to everything they know and experience. Naturally, whenever the Church proclaims the message properly, it will help the faithful in the task of achieving the necessary synthesis between faith and modern knowledge. But when it comes to carrying out this synthesis in their conscience, the Christian person is faced with many problems to which they need to give a personal solution. They will have to distinguish between a greater or a lesser obligation in the teaching of the Church and the theological tradition. They cannot and must not reject the whole faith of the Church, including its definitively binding teachings, even if they are, for example, a paleontologist in 1910 fully convinced of the biological connection between men and the animal kingdom. At that time, this doctrine was rejected by the ecclesiastical magisterium, although not in a definite binding way.

The believer must have a certain knowledge of the "hierarchy of truths" mentioned earlier (ch. 3). They must know that the convictions of their faith are fundamental, central, and existentially significant to deepen them evermore; and not to deny the secondary teachings, but to place them so that they dialogue with them, even to the point of disregard if it's the case. One can maintain both scientific-profane knowledge and a doctrine of faith without realizing its positive compatibility. It should not be said, hastily and arrogantly, that this or that doctrine of faith clearly contradicts a certain knowledge of modern science, and therefore must be rejected. Patience to maintain this truce and await peace with a positive sign is something that belongs today to the maturity of the faith of formed Christians.

Conflicts of maturity also occur in the field of marriage and ecclesiastical law. If anyone knows, before God and their conscience examined with honesty, that their marriage is invalid also according to the general doctrine of the Church but cannot demonstrate it before the ecclesiastical forum and is not authorized to contract a new marriage, they can then remarry only in a civil forum and are also justified before God.

Maturity is something very different from arbitrariness or subjective whim. As it really should be, it makes the human being in a certain sense lonely, without the desired institutional support. They must decide for themselves without being told beforehand what needs to be done. When they thus surrender to themselves, they are not abandoned but situated before God with the verdict in the solitude of their conscience. They must pray and seek the lights and the divine signs. They must have the courage to assume this adult responsibility. Coming of age, concludes Rahner, is a burden of responsibility. It is an elevated task in the process of maturing the Christian and part of the liberation of their freedom toward fullness, which is God's grace.

The example of the paleontologist in 1910, convinced of the biological connection between men and the animal kingdom, is related to the teaching of the Church in the time of Pope Pius X when one could not exclude the literal historical meaning of the first three chapters of the Book of Genesis.[25] There is the account of the creation of plants, animals, and humanity itself, in a distinct and finished way, excluding any evolution of species. The paleontologist in this case should not reject all the faith and all the teachings of the Church but discern in the "hierarchy of truths" what is essential, what is relevant, and what is not. One should never put things in terms of everything or nothing.

This paleontologist's dilemma is not the only one. In the nineteenth century, popes publicly opposed America's independence, the loss of the dominions of the Papal States in Italy, the freedom of conscience and the press, the separation of church and state, and religious freedom. At the beginning of the twentieth century, Pope Pius X argued that, according to the order established by God, there must be princes and vassals, nobles, and commoners, and wise and ignorant.[26] Those who disagreed with these, and other positions, experienced strong conflicts. There were even punishments and excommunications. Many left the Church voluntarily or were forced to leave. To disagree righteously and remain in it was and is a spiritual and humanly arduous task.

A few decades after Karl Rahner published his article on the mature Christian, Rome released a document on the sense of the faith of the faithful, "*Sensus Fidei* in the Life of the Church," authored by the International Theological Commission, subordinate to the Congregation for the Doctrine of the Faith. This document in broad lines confirms Rahner's intuitions. Based on the Scriptures and the tradition of the Church, on the anointing that comes from Christ and teaches everything (cf. 1 John 2:20–27), it is affirmed that the faithful have an instinct for the truth of the Gospel, intrinsically linked to the gift of faith. There is a connaturality that the virtue of faith establishes between the believer and the authentic object of faith, knowledge by empathy or through the heart. As its name indicates (*sensos* in the original), it is very like a natural, immediate, and spontaneous reaction, comparable to a vital instinct or a kind of smell, by which the believer spontaneously adheres to what is according to the truth of faith and avoids what is opposed.[27]

The sense of the faith of the faithful also enables them to distinguish between what is essential to the Catholic faith and what is merely accidental in preachings, or even indifferent to the heart of faith. Thanks to this sense and supported by the prudence given by the Spirit, the believer can perceive, in new historical and cultural contexts, what can be the most appropriate means to give authentic witness to the truth of Jesus Christ, and in Him conform their actions.

This sense offers intuitions that make it possible to open safe paths amid the uncertainties and ambiguities of history, as well as an ability to examine with attention and discernment what human culture and the progress of science have to say. This sense guides the faith life and authentic Christian action. Amid these uncertainties and ambiguities, it may take a long time for this process of discernment to reach a conclusion. In the face of new circumstances, the lay faithful, theologians, and pastors each have their own role to play. It is necessary to show patience and respect in their mutual relations, to reach a clarification of the sense of faith, and to achieve a true consensus of the faithful, an agreement between pastors and the faithful.[28]

What is less known, as this Roman document states, is the role played by the laity related to the development of the Church's moral teaching. It is important to reflect on this role to discern what the Christian conception of proper human behavior is, according to the Gospel. In some areas, the Church's teaching has developed because of the discovery of the requirements demanded in the face of new situations made by the lay faithful. Both the reflection of theologians and the judgment of the bishops' magisterium were based on the Christian experience, already enlightened by the intuitions of these faithful.

Some examples illustrate this role of the sense of the faithful in the development of moral doctrine. The first is the prohibition of clerics and laymen receiving interest on a loan. This prohibition began at the Synod of Elvira, held around the year 306, and lasted for over fifteen hundred years—until 1830. There was clearly a development in the doctrine due to the emergence of a new sensitivity among the laity involved in business, as well as a new reflection of theologians on the nature of money. The second example is the Church's openness to social problems, manifested especially in Pope Leo XIII's encyclical *Rerum Novarum* (1891), which was the result of a slow preparation in which lay Catholics, men of action and thought, played a leading role as "social pioneers." The third example is the change of the Church's position on religious freedom, which was condemned along with the liberal theses in the *Syllabus of Errors* (1864) of Pope Pius IX and later accepted in the *Declaration on Religious Freedom* (1965) of the Second Vatican Council. The International Theological Commission acknowledges that this development would not have been possible without the commitment of many Christians in the fight for human rights.[29]

Countless adult Christians are acting according to their conscience before God, without ecclesial support, but decisively contributing to the good of society and the Church. The Holy Spirit acts in their hearts. Divine Providence acts in these ways.

In the reception of the teaching of the magisterium by the faithful, there are occasions when difficulties and resistance arise. The Roman document urges that in such situations both sides must act appropriately. The faithful should reflect on the teaching given to them, doing their best to understand and accept it. Resisting in principle the teaching of the magisterium is incompatible with an authentic sense of the faith. The magisterium, in turn, must reflect on the teaching transmitted and examine whether there is a need to clarify or reformulate to communicate its essential message more effectively. These mutual efforts in times of difficulty express communion, essential to the life of the Church, as well as the aspiration to receive the grace of the Spirit who guides the Church "into all the truth" (John 16:13). In some cases, the lack of reception may be a sign that some decisions were taken by the authorities without considering the experience and sense of the faith of the faithful, or without the magisterium having sufficiently consulted the faithful.[30]

All this helps to deal with changes in society, with evolution in the doctrine of the Church, and with conflicts between personal consciousness and institution. The struggle of many Christians for human rights was fundamental to reaching an ecumenical council proclaiming religious freedom. The fight for human rights and citizenship of the LGBTQ+ population must also involve Christians so that there is due reception and esteem for this population in the Church.

Queer studies also pave the way within theology. Biblical interpretation has been one of the central issues in excluding positions of various churches as well as in common sense regarding homosexuality. For a long time, it has served to keep the gay community away from contact with the Bible and Bible study, as well as from living in their religious communities. This is so ingrained and has such a long and robust history that the author Rembert Truluck suggests ways to respond, according to the title of his book, *Steps to Recovery from Bible Abuse*.[31] These are actions so that homosexual people can approach the Bible, making it an instrument of liberation and a source of knowledge, for a healthy and guiding spiritual experience. They can also help transgender people. Here are the steps:

1. Admit that you were hurt by religion.
2. Turn to God for help.
3. Examine your faith.
4. Face and deal with your anger.
5 Avoid negative people and churches.
6. Confront the Scriptures used against you.
7. Find supportive and positive Scriptures.
8. Read and study the Gospels.
9. Come out and accept yourself.
10. Develop your support system.
11. Learn to share your faith.
12. Become a missionary of freedom.
13. Give yourself time to heal and recover.

The reality of LGBTQ+ is complex and delicate, brings urgent appeals, and is a challenge to evangelization. The critical reading of Sacred Scripture, due attention to the results of the sciences, the different shades of morality, and fidelity to one's own conscience are elements of the Church's teaching that constitute a rich and dynamic content in the life of the faithful. These elements, combined with theology and spirituality, can greatly help the evangelizing action with that population. One should not seek in the teaching of the Church, not even in the Bible, an instruction manual of an appliance or a complete, universal, and immutable moral code. Decontextualized quotations from the Bible and undue simplifications of the doctrine are often made, with extreme rigidity and a terrible condemnatory impetus directed at LGBTQ+ people. Some speak of the "texts of terror" or "Bible bullets" (see ch. 3) used against these people. Preaching, instead of healing wounds and warming the heart, brings more devastation, and the word of the God of life becomes the word of death. One should never treat these people as being demonized and in need of an exorcism, nor submit them to the prayer of "healing and liberation" to change their sexual orientation or gender identity.

There are different types of apostolates for LGBTQ+ people in the Catholic Church today. One of them is the group called Courage, supported by the United States Conference of Catholic Bishops. It discourages homosexuals from first defining themselves by their sexual inclination, as well as participating in "gay subcultures" that tend to promote a lifestyle considered immoral.[32] There are other groups whose emphasis is on LGBTQ+ inclusion and citizenship in the Church and society, healing of wounds, growth in faith, and respect for conscience in life choices. These groups make up the Global Network of Rainbow Catholics (GNRC).[33] The Diocese of Westminster (England), which covers the city of London, has the LGBT Chaplaincy for the pastoral care of these faithful. The Archdiocese of Santiago, Chile, and the Diocese of Nova Iguaçu, Rio de Janeiro, Brazil, have the Pastoral of Diversity.

In Pope Francis's message to theologians, urging them to continue the path of the Second Vatican Council and to take on the conflicts that affect everyone, this challenge also appears: "Do not settle for a desktop theology. Your place for reflection is the frontier. Do not fall into the temptation to embellish, to add fragrance, to adjust them to some degree and domesticate them."[34] Beyond geographical boundaries, there are also social, ecclesial, and intellectual boundaries that are places of conflict. It is not possible to avoid or control them completely. Many Christians throughout history have inhabited this place and bring an invaluable contribution to the Church. LGBTQ+ and their allies, inside or outside the Church, also inhabit this place. May they bring to the Church and society an equally invaluable contribution.

6

CONCLUDING COMMENTS

The relationship of the LGBTQ+ population with society and the Church over time bears some resemblance to the history of the Jewish people in the Christian era. Hostility to both has been frequently connected. An important example of this is visible in the hatreds spawned by Nazism, which still have strength today. Pope Francis spoke about this at the Vatican with around six hundred participants in an international congress on criminal law:

> I admit that when I hear some speeches, by someone in charge of those who keep order in society or of the government, I am reminded of Hitler's speeches in 1934 and 1936. Today they are actions typical of Nazism which, with its persecution of Jews, gypsies, persons with a homosexual orientation, represents the negative model par excellence of the throwaway culture and the culture of hatred. This is what was done at that time and today these things are being done again. It is necessary to be vigilant, both in the civil and ecclesial spheres, in order to avoid any possible compromise—that is presumed to be involuntary—with these degenerations.[1]

Nazi hatred against these populations was based on the myth of the Aryan race, in which a supposedly superior race should inhabit Germany, eliminating individuals and people considered dangerous and harmful. In those years, there was also a certain anti-Semitism in

Brazil. In 1937, the Brazilian government released a plot on power seizure attributed to communists, contained in a plan with a Jewish name: the "Cohen Plan." It was a government farce to establish the dictatorship of the *Estado Novo* (New State). The fear of the alleged Jewish conspirator allied to communism undermined democracy and paved the way for authoritarianism.

This hatred of the Jews dates to a very distant past, long before Nazism. There are even roots of it in the New Testament, in which collective and hereditary guilt is attributed to these people for the death of Jesus Christ: "His blood be on us and on our children" (Matt 27:25). The Gospels of Matthew and Luke consider the destruction of Jerusalem and its temple in 70 CE a divine punishment for this death.

Christian tradition consolidated the image of the Jew as a deicidal people (who killed God). For many centuries in the Latin liturgy of Good Friday, the "perfidious Jews" were prayed for. Originally thought of as perfidious nonbelievers, common sense soon associated them with traitors. They were harassed by simple people, confined in ghettos, and massacred by crusaders, as well as by penitents. They were expelled from kingdoms and persecuted by the Inquisition. In the sixteenth century, Martin Luther wrote against the Jews, proposing to burn the synagogues and ban Jewish worship on pain of death. Nazi Germany reissued these writings, with a circulation of millions of copies.

Modern anti-Semitism and Nazism are secular, alien, and even in conflict with the Christian religion. However, there were undeniably points of convergence. Only in the 1960s, with the Second Vatican Council, the Catholic world reconsidered the alleged Jewish guilt for Jesus's death. Since then, the Jewish people must not be presented in the preaching and catechesis of the Church as a people cursed by God. This is an example of the ecclesial vigilance mentioned by the pope to avoid compromise with such degeneration.

The Nazi persecution of gays, in turn, also dates to a distant past, as we have seen (see ch. 2). German laws before Nazism already criminalized homosexual practice, but Hitler's regime acted with ruthless and cruel rigor: he sent thousands of homosexuals to concentration camps, dressed them in a prison uniform with a pink triangle, subjected them to the execration and violence of the other prisoners, as well as to medical experiments with devastating effects. And furthermore, the end of Nazism didn't change their luck. The Allied military government kept homosexuals incarcerated to continue serving time, unlike other prisoners. Homosexuality remained criminalized in Germany—a situation that only began to change in the 1970s.

Today, about seventy countries still criminalize the practice of homosexuality. Some punish it with death. Not long ago, I heard the dramatic account of an African person about the wicked alliance of Catholics, Evangelicals, and Muslims in their country to arrest and beat up LGBTQ+ people. Even in Brazil, where homotransphobia was recently criminalized, there are still sad and abundant examples of physical and verbal violence. Many still consider LGBTQ+ people to be harmful and dangerous, as were Jews in the past, and they see gender studies as a branch of family-threatening communism.

Vigilance to avoid compromise with such degeneration requires a broad review of doctrinal practices, preaching, and formulations in the Christian world, just as it was done for the Jews. Much remains to be done. May Pope Francis's warning be a promising impetus.

The reinterpretation of tradition from an inclusive perspective must also contemplate the family environment. One of the fundamental references to the Christian imagination is the Holy Family—Jesus, Mary, and Joseph. At Christmastime, we also celebrate the family in which Jesus was born and which is elevated to an exemplary level. The liturgical celebration proposes it as a model, whose virtues must be imitated. It is a family consisting of a heterosexual, monogamous, and indissoluble union. But what about the other family configurations, so numerous in society today, including LGBTQ+ unions?

Taking the Holy Family as a fundamental reference, we should reflect on the genealogy of Jesus presented in the Gospels. For us today, that list of names may seem unnecessary and make no sense. But there are important and even surprising aspects. In the biblical world, the mention of sonship was the mark of identity, for example: Joshua, son of Nun; Simon, son of Jonah; and James and John, sons of Zebedee. Two genealogies of Jesus are presented: In Matthew (1:1–17) and Luke (3:23–38). The lineage is all paternal and masculine, according to the patriarchal character of society. In Matthew, the list of names goes to Abraham, as it is announced in the beginning: "An account of the genealogy of Jesus the Messiah, the son of David, the son of Abraham."

With this, Jesus binds himself to the great king, David, and to the patriarch of the Hebrews and the father of believers, Abraham.

There's something very original about Matthew's genealogy. He mentions four women. He didn't have to mention them since Luke didn't. The four women mentioned by Matthew could have been the so-called four mothers of Israel: Sarah, Rebecca, Leah, and Rachel; wives of the patriarchs Abraham, Isaac, and Jacob respectively. But no. Tamar, Raab, Ruth, and "the woman of Uriah" (Bathsheba) are the ones mentioned. Who are these women?

Tamar was married to Onan, who was punished by God with death for doing *coitus interuptus*. According to the law, Tamar was to marry a brother of Onan to beget descendants in the family of her deceased husband. But her father-in-law, the patriarch Judah, did not give her his son Shelah, with whom she was to marry. So, Tamar disguised herself as a prostitute and seduced her father-in-law, becoming pregnant with his child. After the whole story came to light, Judah acknowledged, "She is more in the right than I, since I did not give her to my son Shelah" (Gen 38:26).

Rahab was a prostitute in Jericho at the time of the conquest of Canaan. She protected Joshua's spies. When the city was taken by the Israelites, its inhabitants were decimated, but Rahab and her family were spared in return for their collaboration that was decisive for the Israelite victory. Ruth was a foreigner, a threat to the Hebrew people by the danger of mixed marriages and pagan customs (cf. Ps 106:34–41). Uriah's wife was the person with whom David committed adultery. She became pregnant, and after that, David plotted the death of her husband, who was a member of the royal army. The plot succeeded, and Uriah died in battle.

In this way, Matthew presents to us Jesus, son of David and son of Abraham, as the son of Tamar, Rahab, Ruth, and Bathsheba; one who disguised herself, a prostitute, a foreigner, and someone who committed adultery. With this, Matthew prepares the reader of the Gospel for what he will say next: "When his mother Mary had been engaged to Joseph, but before they lived together, she was found to be with child from the Holy Spirit" (1:18). Therefore, God is surprising and disconcerting. From the long saga of Israel, with its grandeur and misery, He gave birth to the Messiah, using various human and family situations. In the origins of the Holy Family, therefore, other family configurations are mentioned.

Fortunately, today some space is opening for those who live in these other settings. As already noted (see ch. 3), the Brazilian bishops recognize that people united without the rite of marriage participate in parishes, as well as others in second unions or same-sex unions. Some live alone supporting their children, grandparents who raise grandchildren, uncles and aunts who provide for nephews and nieces, and children who are adopted by single people. The bishops affirm the challenge of "welcoming, guiding, and including in communities" rather than edicting prohibitions. Among the listed configurations, certainly, the one that finds more resistance is still the same-sex union. The exhortation *Amoris Laetitia* greatly contributes to the acceptance of all by recognizing that even in a situation considered irregular, one can live in the grace of God and receive the help of the Church that does not necessarily exclude the sacraments (see ch. 3).

The families of origin of LGBTQ+ people also need help. Most of their parents dreamed of cisgender and heterosexual children, who would marry people of the opposite sex and thus give them grandchildren. When this expectation does not materialize, they are often dismayed. It is something similar to mourning. The son or daughter you dreamed of no longer exists. Living with this harsh reality requires patience and openness. We must exhort them that children, whatever they may be, are always a gift of God the Creator to parents and humanity, as well as the life of any human being. And parents are an instrument of divine Providence for them so that they have life, affection, education, and values.

Having LGBTQ+ children brings them to the complex reality of sexual and gender diversity. Society and families are looking for reasonable ways to deal with this, including the Christian world and the Catholic Church that are also part of society. No human being is merely an LGBTQ+ person but first, rather, a creature of God and recipient of God's grace that makes them God's child and heir of eternal life.

Movies and videos can also help these parents. One of them is very emblematic and recommendable based on the book of the same name, *Prayers for Bobby*, by Leroy Aarons,[2] and released on American TV in 2009. The film tells the true story of Mary Griffith, played by actress Sigourney Weaver. Mary is a regretful Presbyterian mother trying to cure her homosexual son, who ended up killing himself as a result of such bullying. The drama takes place in the 1980s in the town of Walnut Creek, California. On August 27, 1983, Bobby Griffith took his life at the age of twenty by jumping off an overpass over a highway in Portland, Oregon, to where he had moved.

For years, he suffered harsh pressure from his family to overcome his homosexuality. His mother, a fervent religious, did not admit to her son's homosexuality, which she considered to be a disease and an abomination, and used the Bible to support her convictions. Bobby kept a journal, recording questions to God and phrases of self-denial based on the teachings he received. This record reveals how his religiosity in a Church that condemned him to hell and the lack of family support were crucial in his decision to end his life.

Years before his death, Bobby had made an unsuccessful suicide attempt. Very shaken, he ended up revealing his homosexuality to his brother. The brother made it known to the mother, and so the homophobic harassment began. She only realized that her son did not choose to be gay when he died and she researched homosexuality, something she regretted not having done before. Mary became an activist in an association of family and friends of gays and lesbians. To the parents, she gives a message: "I have spoken to many parents in these years. And I think all I can tell them is to listen to their children and try not to make your opinions prevail over theirs."

Eight months after her son's death, Mary gave a deposition at the city council meeting, where the institution of a day to celebrate gay freedom was voted. This testimony became one of the most striking and moving moments of the film.

> Homosexuality is a sin. Homosexuals are doomed to spend eternity in hell. If they wanted to change, they could be healed of their evil ways. If they would turn away from temptation, they could be normal again if only they would try and try harder if it doesn't work. These are all the things I said to my son Bobby when I found out he was gay.
>
> When he told me he was homosexual my world fell apart. I did everything I could to cure him of his sickness. Eight months ago my son jumped off a bridge and killed himself. I deeply regret my lack of knowledge about gay and lesbian people. I see that everything I was taught and told was bigotry and dehumanizing slander. If I had investigated beyond what I was told, if I had just listened to my son when he poured his heart out to me, I would not be standing here

today with you filled with regret. I believe that God was pleased with Bobby's kind and loving spirit. In God's eyes kindness and love are what it's all about.

I didn't know that each time I echoed eternal damnation for gay people each time I referred to Bobby as sick and perverted and a danger to our children. His self-esteem and sense of worth were being destroyed. And finally, his spirit broke beyond repair. It was not God's will that Bobby climbed over the side of a freeway overpass and jumped directly into the path of an eighteen-wheel truck which killed him instantly. Bobby's death was the direct result of his parent's ignorance and fear of the word gay.

He wanted to be a writer. His hopes and dreams should not have been taken from him, but they were. There are children, like Bobby, sitting in your congregations. Unknown to you they will be listening as you echo "amen" and that will soon silence their prayers. Their prayers to God for understanding and acceptance and for your love but your hatred and fear and ignorance of the word gay will silence those prayers. So, before you echo "amen" in your home and place of worship. Think. Think and remember a child is listening.[3]

This story bears much resemblance to so many others experienced by LGBTQ+ people and their families. Homotransphobia kills, and when it doesn't, it can hurt deeply. Such hostility is often associated with religion, conveying an image of God that brings irreparable devastation. In this case, the hard work of the Christian theologian is urgently needed to distinguish the message of life from its form of transmission, from the cultural elements in which this message was codified at a given time, as taught by Pope Francis. Not doing this exercise of discernment inevitably leads to betraying the content of the message. It makes the good news, the true meaning of the Gospel, no longer new and no longer good, becoming a sterile word, empty of all its creative, healing, and resuscitating force. This is how the faith of the people of our time becomes endangered (see ch. 3). In the story of Bobby Griffith, we have a full and tragic example of this neglect and where the good news has become terrible news. Its creative, healing, and resuscitating force has been transformed into relentless oppression and lethal poison.

In the Judeo-Christian tradition, however, there are many inspiring accounts and positive images of God's love for humanity and creation. One of the most beautiful is that of the origin of the rainbow in Genesis, the first book of the Bible. This book was written during the Jewish exile in Babylon, in the sixth century BCE. It is a monotheistic retelling of ancient Babylonian myths about the creation of the world and the flood. In Genesis, after the universal flood in the time of Noah, God establishes an eternal covenant with humanity and with creation, whose sign is the rainbow:

> "When I bring clouds over the earth and the bow is seen in the clouds, I will remember my covenant that is between me and you and every living creature of all flesh; and the waters shall never again become a flood to destroy all flesh. When the bow is in the clouds, I will see it and remember the everlasting covenant between God and every living creature of all flesh that is on the earth." God said to Noah, "This is the sign of the covenant that I have established between me and all flesh that is on the earth." (Gen 9:14–17)

In this account, the destruction of the world and its living beings is neither divine desire nor design, even if, according to ancient cosmology, this has ever happened. God is Creator, God of life, who wants the good of creation in the widest diversity of his beings.

More than two millennia after Genesis, the LGBTQ+ movement has adopted the rainbow flag as its symbol. This started in 1978, in San Francisco, with the artist Gilbert Baker, who made a model with eight colors. On June 25 of that year, Gay Freedom Day in the United States, the first versions of the flag were seen on the streets. Then the model was simplified, becoming six colors. The artist explained that his idea was to promote the idea of diversity and inclusion, using "something of nature to represent that our sexuality is a human right."[4]

At that time, Brazil lived under the yoke of the civil-military dictatorship. The archbishop of Olinda and Recife, Hélder Câmara, had become an extraordinary defender of the poor and human rights, suffering severe censorship and persecution by the regime. Despite this, he managed to publish a book of poetry. By coincidence, it was also in the year 1978, and one of these poems was:

> MAKE ME A RAINBOW
> that welcomes all colors
> in which your light
> is fragmented!
> Make me, always more,
> like a rainbow
> that announces the calm
> after the storms.[5]

Hélder's rainbow and that of LGBTQ+ people belong to very different contexts but have elements in common. Both defend human rights, diversity, and inclusion. All people are the image and likeness of God in this world, colors in which divine light is fragmented in the diversity of creation. May they enjoy the calm after the storm and shine with all their radiance.

NOTES

INTRODUCTION

1. Pope Francis, "General Audience," Saint Peter's Square, Wednesday, February 26, 2014, https://www.vatican.va/content/francesco/en/audiences/2014/documents/papa-francesco_20140226_udienza-generale.html.

2. Pope Francis, "Address of His Holiness Pope Francis to Participants in the Meeting Promoted by the Pontifical Council for Promoting the New Evangelization," Synod Hall, Wednesday, October 11, 2017, https://www.vatican.va/content/francesco/en/speeches/2017/october/documents/papa-francesco_20171011_convegno-nuova-evangelizzazione.html.

CHAPTER 1

1. See Yves Congar, *La tradition et la vie de l'Église* (Paris: Cerf, 1984), 6.

2. Not unlike creationism, fixism holds that the species are always what they have been since their creation.

3. OCQ (Office de catéchèse du Québec). *La force des rencontres. Homme et femme il les créa* (Montréal: Fides, 1976), n. 6. In Guy Durand, *Sexualidade e fé: Síntese de teologia moral* (São Paulo: Loyola, 1989).

4. Antônio Moser, "Apenas questão de gênero?" *Revista Eclesiástica Brasileira* 76, no. 301 (2016): 44–74, https://doi.org/10.29386/reb.v76i301.233.

5. Todd A. Salzman and Michael G. Lawler, *The Sexual Person: Toward a Renewed Catholic Anthropology*, Moral Traditions (Washington, DC: Georgetown University Press, 2008), 40.

6. See Jean Delumeau, *Sin and Fear: The Emergence of the Western Guilt Culture, 13th–18th Centuries*, trans. Eric Nicholson (New York: St. Martin's Press, 1990).

7. Demosthenes, *Against Neaera*, Dem. 59 122. See *Demosthenes*, trans. Norman W. DeWitt, and Norman J. DeWitt (Cambridge, MA: Harvard University Press, 1949).

8. Salzman and Lawler, *Sexual Person*, 31–32.

9. Salzman and Lawler, *Sexual Person*, 32–33, 42.

10. See Marciano Vidal, *Sexualidade e condição homossexual na moral cristã* (Aparecida, SP, Brazil: Santuário, 2008), 12–16.

11. See Vidal, *Sexualidade e condição homossexual*, 19–20.

12. See Vidal, *Sexualidade e condição homossexual*, 21–22.

13. See Salzman and Lawler, *Sexual Person*, 44–46.

14. See Vidal, *Sexualidade e condição homossexual*, 23–24.

15. Luís Corrêa Lima, "Divorciados recasados diante dos sacramentos," *Revista Eclesiástica Brasileira* 60, no. 239 (2000): 641–49, https://revistaeclesiasticabrasileira.itf.edu.br/reb/article/view/2162.

16. See Salzman and Lawler, *Sexual Person*, 47–49.

17. See Salzman and Lawler, *Sexual Person*, 39.

18. See Pope Pius XI, *Casti Connubii*, encyclical letter on Christian marriage, Rome, December 31, 1930, no. 10, https://www.vatican.va/content/pius-xi/en/encyclicals/documents/hf_p-xi_enc_19301231_casti-connubii.html.

19. See Vidal, *Sexualidade e condição homossexual*, 25–27, 103.

20. See Vidal, *Sexualidade e condição homossexual*, 28–35.

21. See Cardeal Carlo M. Martini and Georg Sporschill, *Diálogos noturnos em Jerusalém: Sobre o risco da fé* (São Paulo: Paulus; Rio de Janeiro: PUC-Rio, 2008), 122–23.

22. St. Justin Martyr, *First and Second Apologies*, Ancient Christian Writers (Mahwah, NJ: Paulist Press, 1997), 45.

23. See Salzman and Lawler, *Sexual Person*, 54–55.

24. Lactantius, *The Divine Institutes*, VI, 23.

25. See Vidal, *Sexualidade e condição homossexual*, 38–44.

26. St. Augustine, *De bono coniugali*, PL 40, 380.

27. St. Augustine, *De bono coniugali*, PL 40, 377–78.

28. St. Augustine, *The City of God*, XIV, 24.

29. St. Augustine, *The City of God*, XXII, 24.

30. See *Catechism of the Catholic Church*, 1997, n. 390, 398–400.

31. See Delumeau, *Sin and Fear*, 77–94.

32. See Delumeau, *Sin and Fear*, 31.

33. Jean Comby, *From the Beginnings to the Fifteenth Century*, vol. 1 of *How to Read Church History* (New York: Crossroad, 1985), 144.

34. Lotario dei Segni (Pope Innocent III), *De miseria condicionis humane*, ed. Robert E. Lewis (Athens: The University of Georgia Press, 1978), 93, 99.

35. Thomas à Kempis, *Imitation of Christ* I: 2, 22, (Milwaukee: The Bruce Publishing Company, 1940), 4, 37, https://www.ccel.org/ccel/kempis/imitation.all.html.

36. See Delumeau, *Sin and Fear*, 49–50.

37. Venerable Louis of Granada, *The Sinner's Guide*, trans. Fr. Charles Hyancinth McKenna (Charlotte, NC: TAN Books, 2014), 233.

38. See Salzman and Lawler, *Sexual Person*, 63–66.

39. See Vidal, *Sexualidade e condição homossexual*, 54–59.

40. See Vidal, *Sexualidade e condição homossexual*, 40–42.

41. Marc Oraison, *Reconciliación: Memorias* (Salamanca: Sígueme, 1969), 195.

42. See Salzman and Lawler, *Sexual Person*, 275–79.

43. See Pope Pius XI, *Casti Connubii*, encyclical letter on Christian marriage, Rome, 1930, no. 24. Available at: https://www.vatican.va/content/pius-xi/en/encyclicals/documents/hf_p-xi_enc_19301231_casti-connubii.html.

44. Pope Pius XII, *Divino Afflante Spiritu*, encyclical letter on promoting biblical studies, Rome, September 30, 1943, no. 20. Available at: https://www.vatican.va/content/pius-xii/en/encyclicals/documents/hf_p-xii_enc_30091943_divino-afflante-spiritu.html.

45. See Benedict XVI, *Verbum Domini*, post-synodal exhortation, September 30, 2010, nos. 7–9. Available at: https://www.vatican.va/content/benedict-xvi/en/apost_exhortations/documents/hf_ben-xvi_exh_20100930_verbum-domini.html.

46. See Benedict XVI, *Caritas in Veritate*, encyclical letter, June 29, 2009, no. 51. Available at: https://www.vatican.va/content/benedict-xvi/en/encyclicals/documents/hf_ben-xvi_enc_20090629_caritas-in-veritate.html.

47. See Benedict XVI, "Address of His Holiness Benedict XVI to the Participants in the International Congress on Natural Moral Law," Rome, February 12, 2007, https://www.vatican.va/content/benedict-xvi/en/speeches/2007/february/documents/hf_ben-xvi_spe_20070212_pul.html.

48. ITC (International Theological Commission), "In Search of a Universal Ethic: A New Look at the Natural Law," Rome, 2009, nos. 10, 59, 113, https://www.vatican.va/roman_curia/congregations/cfaith/cti_documents/rc_con_cfaith_doc_20090520_legge-naturale_en.html.

49. Bernhard Häring, "Sessualità," in *Dizionario enciclopedico di teologia morale*, ed. L. Rossi and A. Valsecchi (Rome: Paoline, 1973), 925.

50. See *Catechism of the Catholic Church*, 1997, n. 1778.

51. See Salzman and Lawler, *Sexual Person*, 72–75, 283.

52. See Pope John XXIII, *Pacem in Terris*, encyclical letter, Rome, April 11, 1963, nos. 41, 140, https://www.vatican.va/content/john-xxiii/en/encyclicals/documents/hf_j-xxiii_enc_11041963_pacem.html; see also *Gaudium et Spes*, 9.

53. Heinrich Denzinger, *Enchiridion Symbolorum: Compendium of Creeds, Definitions, and Declarations on Matters of Faith and Morals*, ed. Peter Hünermann (San Francisco: Ignatius Press, 2012), n. 3148.

54. See Pope Pius XI, *Casti Connubii*, nos. 20–21.

55. See Pope Pius XII, *Moral Questions Affecting Married Life: The Apostolate of the Midwife* (New York: Paulist Press, 1951), nos. 24–25.

56. See Pope Paul VI, *Humanae Vitae*, encyclical letter, Rome, July 25, 1968, nos. 11, 14, https://www.vatican.va/content/paul-vi/en/encyclicals/documents/hf_p-vi_enc_25071968_humanae-vitae.html.

57. See Vidal, *Sexualidade e condição homossexual*, 105–6.

58. Joseph Ratzinger, "Hacia una teología del matrimonio," *Selecciones de teologia* 35 (1970): 237–48.

59. See Salzman and Lawler, *Sexual Person*, 101–39.

60. See Salzman and Lawler, *Sexual Person*, 89.

61. Moser, "Apenas questão de gênero?," 60–61.

62. Jean-Yves Calvez, "Morale sociale et morale sexuelle," *Études* 3785 (1993): 641–50.

63. See Vidal, *Sexualidade e condição homossexual*, 88–89.

64. See Benedict XVI, "General Audience," April 26, 2006, https://www.vatican.va/content/benedict-xvi/en/audiences/2006/documents/hf_ben-xvi_aud_20060426.html.

65. Joseph Ratzinger, "The Transmission of Divine Revelation," in *Commentary on the Documents of Vatican II*, vol. 3, ed. Herbert Vorgrimler (New York: Herder and Herder, 1969), 185. Quoted in Salzman and Lawler, *Sexual Person*, 214.

CHAPTER 2

1. Jaqueline Gomes de Jesus, "Orientações sobre identidade de gênero: Conceitos e termos," *Guia técnico sobre pessoas transexuais, travestis e demais transgêneros, para formadores de opinião* 2 (2012).

2. "Introduction," *Yogyakarta Principles*, ARC International. 2016. Available at: https://yogyakartaprinciples.org.

3. OAB (Ordem dos Advogados do Brasil—Conselho Federal [Brazilian Bar Association—Federal Council]), "Anteprojeto estatuto da diversidade sexual e de gênero" [Draft sexual and gender diversity statute], 2017.

4. Paul Veyne, "A homossexualidade em Roma," in *Sexualidades ocidentais*, ed. Philippe Ariès and André Béjin (São Paulo: Brasiliense, 1985), 39–49.

5. John Boswell, *Christianity, Social Tolerance, and Homosexuality: Gay People in Western Europe from the Beginning of the Christian Era to the Fourteenth Century* (Chicago: University of Chicago Press, 2015), 27.

6. See Gabriel Soares de Sousa, *Tratado descritivo do Brasil em 1587* [Descriptive Treatise of Brazil in 1857] (Rio de Janeiro: Laemmert's Universal Typographia, 1851), 308.

7. See Ruth Landes, *The City of Women* (Albuquerque: University of New Mexico Press, [1947] 2006).

8. Marciano Vidal, *Sexualidade e condição homossexual na moral cristã* (Aparecida, SP, Brazil: Santuário, 2008), 126–28.

9. D. Sebastião Monteiro da Vide, *Constituições primeiras do arcebispado da Bahia* [First Constitutions of the Archbishopric of Bahia] (Brasília: Federal Senate, Editorial Board, 2007), 331–32.

10. See Philippine Ordinations, V, XIII. The quote is a translation from Portuguese. The original version is available in *Ordenações*, Quinto Livro, 1162–1163, https://www2.senado.leg.br/bdsf/bitstream/handle/id/242733/000010186_05.pdf?sequence=33&isAllowed=y.

11. See John Boswell, *Same-Sex Unions in Pre-modern Europe* (New York: Vintage, 1995).

12. Gil Aznar and R. Federico, "Las parejas no casadas: Nota a propósito de algunas publicaciones recientes," *Revista española de derecho canónico* 53 (1996): 819–22.

13. Marcello de Carvalho Azevedo, SJ, *Entroncamentos e entrechoques: Vivendo a fé em um mundo plural* (São Paulo, Loyola, 1991), 101–3.

14. Jean-Claude Féray, "Une histoire critique du mot homosexualité," *Revue Arcadie* (March–April 1981). Available at: http://culture-et-debats.over-blog.com/article-histoire-critique-homosexualite-par-jean-claude-feray-61410181.html.

15. Bernardino Leers and José Antonio Trasferetti, *Homossexuais e ética cristã* (Campinas, SP, Brazil: Átomo, 2002), 89–90.

16. Boswell, *Christianity, Social Tolerance, and Homosexuality*, 453.

17. See James Naylor Green and Ronald Polito, *Frescos trópicos: Fontes sobre a homossexualidade masculina no Brasil (1870–1980)* (Rio de Janeiro: José Olympio, 2006), 104–12.

18. See Norberto Bobbio, *A era dos direitos* (Rio de Janeiro: Campus, 1992), 1–10, 34.

19. Boswell, *Christianity, Social Tolerance, and Homosexuality*, 452, 454.

20. Suzana Herculano-Houzel, "O cérebro homosexual," *Folha de São Paulo* 165 (July 2006): 46–51.

21. Joan Roughgarden, "Homossexualidade como traço adaptativo," *Mente & cérebro* 185 (2008): 54–55.

22. Amigos & Tribos, repost of Julio Lancellotti (n.d.), Facebook, June 10, 2015. Available at: https://www.facebook.com/photo?fbid=666055623525398&set=a.148340121963620.

23. See Kenji Yoshino, *Covering: The Hidden Assault on Our Civil Rights* (New York: Random House, 2006).

24. H. A. R. Irigaray, "Gays no mundo corporativo: Rompendo o pacto do silencio," *O social em questão* 20 (2008): 113.

25. Gomes de Jesus, *Orientações sobre identidade de gênero*, 30.

26. See C. Mancina, "Simone de Beauvoir mãe do feminismo," *L'Osservatore Romano*, September 1, 2016. Available at: https://www.osservatoreromano.va/pt.html.

27. See Simone de Beauvoir, *The Ethics of Ambiguity* (New York: Open Road Media, 2018), 16.

28. See Helena Vieira, "Teoria queer, o que é isso?" *Fórum*, June 7, 2015. Available at: https://revistaforum.com.br.

29. Berenice Bento, "Queer o que? Ativismo e estudos transviados," *Cult* 193 (2014): 45.

30. Stuart Hall, *A identidade cultural na pós-modernidade* (Rio de Janeiro: DP&A, 2001), 9, 46.

31. Judith Butler, *Gender Trouble: Feminism and the Subversion of Identity* (New York: Routledge, 2006), 28, 30.

32. Butler, *Gender Trouble*, 47–48.

33. Butler, *Gender Trouble*, 45–46.

34. Butler, *Gender Trouble*, 8.

35. Butler, *Gender Trouble*, 209–11.

36. Judith Butler, "Como os corpos se tornam matéria: Entrevista com Judith Butler," interview by Baukje Prins and Irene Costera Meijerby, *Estudos feministas* 10, no. 1 (2002): 157.

37. Judith Butler, "La invención de la palabra," interview by Milagros Belgrano Rawson, *Pagina 12*, May 8, 2009. Available at: https://www.pagina12.com.ar/diario/suplementos/soy/1-742-2009-05-08.html.

38. R. Pompeu, "Questionário para heterossexuais," *Caros amigos*, May 2008, https://sapatariadf.wordpress.com/category/mundo-diverso/page/2/.

CHAPTER 3

1. Jaime Snoek, "Eles também são da nossa estirpe: Considerações sobre a homofilia," *Revista Vozes* (September 1967): 792–803. Available at: www.diversidadesexual.com.br.

2. Clarêncio Neotti, "Cem anos da revista de cultura Vozes," *Jornal semanal da Sociedade Brasileira de Estudos Interdisciplinares da Comunicação* 3, no. 68 (2007). Available at: www.intercom.org.br.

3. President Barack Obama, "Inaugural address by President Barack Obama," Washington, January 21, 2013. Available at: https://obamawhitehouse.archives.gov/the-press-office/2013/01/21/inaugural-address-president-barack-obama.

4. Francis DeBernardo, "Supreme court marriage equality case will be led by catholic gay couple," New Ways Ministry, April 21, 2015. Available at: https://www.newwaysministry.org/2015/04/21/supreme-court-marriage-equality-case-will-be-led-by-catholic-gay-couple/.

5. Gaëlle Dupont, "Relator de projeto favorável ao casamento gay na França se diz confiante, apesar de sofrer ameaças," *Boletim eletrônico IHU*, January 30, 2013. Available at: www.ihu.unisinos.br.

6. "Mariage pour tous, un progrès humain," *Témoignage Chrétien*, December 14, 2012. Available at: https://temoignagechretien.fr.

7. Congregation for the Doctrine of the Faith (CDF), "Letter to the Bishops of the Catholic Church on the Pastoral Care of Homosexual Persons—*homosexualitatis problema*," Rome, 1986, nos. 16, 10–11. Available at: www.vatican.va.

8. See "Comunicado del obispo de Cádiz y Ceuta," September 1, 2015. Available at: www.es.catholic.net.

9. CDF, "Some Considerations Concerning the Response to Legislative Proposals on the Non-Discrimination of Homosexual Persons," Rome, July 24, 1992, nos. 10–13. Available at: www.vatican.va.

10. CDF, "Considerations Regarding Proposals to Give Legal Recognition to Unions Between Homosexual Persons," Rome, June 3, 2003, nos. 5, 7–9. Available at: www.vatican.va.

11. Pontifical Council for the Family, "Familia y Derechos Humanos," Vatican City, 1999, nos. 66, 74. Available at: www.vatican.va.

12. CDF, "Letter to the Bishops of the Catholic Church on the Collaboration of Men and Women in the Church and in the World," Rome, May 31, 2004, nos. 2–4. Available at: www.vatican.va.

13. Benedict XVI, "Address of His Holiness Benedict XVI to the Members of the Roman Curia for the Traditional Exchange of Christmas Greetings," Rome, December 22, 2008. Available at: www.vatican.va.

14. Chicago Clergy, "An Open Letter to the Hierarchy of the Roman Catholic Church Regarding the Pastoral Care of Gay and Lesbian Persons," December 19, 2013. Available at: https://www.bishop-accountability.org/resources/resource-files/timeline/2003-12-19-Prendergast-OpenLetter.htm.

15. "Statement of the Holy See Delegation at the 63rd Session of the General Assembly of the United Nations on the Declaration on Human Rights, Sexual Orientation and Gender Identity," December 18, 2008. Available at: www.vatican.va.

16. "Difesa dei diritti e ideología," *L'Osservatore Romano*, December 20, 2008. Available at: https://tuespetrus.wordpress.com/2008/12/19/difesa-dei-diritti-e-ideologia/.

17. USCCB (United States Conference of Catholic Bishops), "Ministry to Persons with a Homosexual Inclination: Guidelines for Pastoral Care," Washington, DC, 2006. Available at: www.usccb.org.

18. USCCB, "Always our Children: a Pastoral Message to Parents of Homosexual Children and Suggestions for Pastoral Ministers," Washington, DC, 1997. Available at: www.usccb.org.

19. CDES (Conference of Swiss Bishops), "Note pastorale 10: position de la Conférence des Évêques Suisses concernant la bénédiction par l'Église de couples homosexuels et l'engagement par l'Église de personnes vivant en partenariat homosexuel." Fribourg, 2002, no. 3. Available at: www.eveques.ch.

20. CEF (Conference of French Bishops), "Élargir le mariage aux personnes de même sexe? Ouvrons le débat!" Paris, 2012. Available at: www.eglise.catholique.fr.

21. CNBB (National Conference of the Bishops of Brazil), *Comunidade de comunidades: uma nova paróquia* (Brasília: Edições CNBB, 2014), nos. 217–18.

22. CES (Catholic Education Service), *Made in God's Image: Challenging Homophobic and Biphobic Bullying in Catholic Schools* (London: St Mary's University, 2018). Available at: www.catholiceducation.org.uk.

23. Pope Francis, "Apostolic Journey to Rio de Janeiro on the Occasion of the XXVIII World Youth Day: Press Conference of Pope Francis during the Return Flight." July 28, 2013. Available at: www.vatican.va.

24. Pope Francis, "Solemnity of Pentecost Holy Mass with the Ecclesial Movements: Homily of Pope Francis," Rome, May 19, 2013. Available at: www.vatican.va.

25. Pope Francis, "Interview with Pope Francis by Fr Antonio Spadaro, editor in chief of the Italian Jesuit magazine *La Civiltà Cattolica*," *L'Osservatore Romano*, September 21, 2013, https://www.vatican

.va/content/francesco/en/speeches/2013/september/documents/papa-francesco_20130921_intervista-spadaro.html.

26. Pope Francis, "Interview with Pope Francis by Fr Antonio Spadaro."

27. Pope Francis, "Interview with Pope Francis by Fr Antonio Spadaro."

28. See Pope Francis, "Address of His Holiness Pope Francis to Participants in the Meeting Promoted by the Pontifical Council for Promoting the New Evangelization," Rome, October 11, 2017. Available at: www.vatican.va.

29. Pope Francis, "Apostolic Journey to Rio de Janeiro."

30. Pope Francis, "Address of His Holiness Pope Francis to Participants in the Convention Sponsored by the Congregation for the Clergy on the 50th Anniversary of the Conciliar Decrees 'Optatam Totius' and 'Presbyterorum Ordinis,'" Rome, November 20, 2015. Available at: www.vatican.va.

31. *Catechism of the Catholic Church*, 1997, n. 2343.

32. Ana B. Hernández, "El bendito encuentro entre Francisco y Diego," *Hoy*, January 25, 2015. Available at: www.hoy.es.

33. Carlos E. Cué, "El Papa me pidió perdón, está espantado con los abusos, esto es un tsunami," *El País*, May 19, 2018. Available at: www.elpais.com.

34. Pope Francis, "In-Flight Press Conference of His Holiness Pope Francis from Azerbaijan to Rome," October 2, 2016. Available at: www.vatican.va.

35. Pope Francis, "Letter of His Holiness Pope Francis to the Grand Chancellor of the 'Pontificia Universidad Católica Argentina' for the 100th Anniversary of the Founding of the Faculty of Theology," March 3, 2015. Available at: www.vatican.va.

36. Pope Francis, "Video Message of His Holiness Pope Francis to Participants in an International Theological Congress Held at the Pontifical Catholic University of Argentina." Buenos Aires, September 1–3, 2015. Available at: www.vatican.va.

37. Pope Francis, "General Audience," April 15, 2015. Available at: www.vatican.va.

38. Pope Francis, "Conclusion of the Synod of Bishops: Address of His Holiness Pope Francis," Rome, October 24, 2015. Available at: www.vatican.va.

39. Benedict XVI, "Carta do santo padre Bento XVI," in *Youcat—Brasil: Catecismo jovem da Igreja Católica* (São Paulo: Paulus, 2011), 6–7.

40. CCE (Congregation for Catholic Education), "'Male and Female He Created Them': Towards a Path of Dialogue on the Question of Gender Theory in Education," Vatican, 2019. Available at: www.vatican.va.

41. PBC (Pontifical Biblical Commission), "'What is Man?' (Psalm 8:5): An Itinerary through Biblical Anthropology," Vatican, 2019. Available at: www.vatican.va.

42. John XXIII, "Solemn Opening of the Second Vatican Council: Address of His Holiness Pope John XXIII," Vatican, October 11, 1962, 4.2–4.3. Available at: https://www.vatican.va/content/john-xxiii/it/speeches/1962/documents/hf_j-xxiii_spe_19621011_opening-council.html.

CHAPTER 4

1. CC (Congregation for the Clergy), "The Gift of the Priestly Vocation," Vatican, 2016, n. 1. Available at: www.clerus.va.

2. See CCE, "Instruction Concerning the Criteria for the Discernment of Vocations with Regard to Persons with Homosexual Tendencies in view of their Admission to the Seminary and to Holy Orders," Vatican, 2005, n. 2. Available at: www.vatican.va. See also CC, "The Gift of the Priestly Vocation," nn. 119–200.

3. CICL (Congregation for Institutes of Consecrated Life and Societies of Apostolic Life), "Directives on Formation in Religious Institutes." Rome, 1990, n. 39. Available at: https://www.vatican.va/roman_curia/congregations/ccscrlife/documents/rc_con_ccscrlife_doc_02021990_directives-on-formation_en.html.

4. Zenon Grocholewski, "Quando não é oportuno admitir ao sacerdócio," *30 dias* 11 (2005): 24–25.

5. CCE, introduction to "Instruction Concerning the Criteria for the Discernment of Vocations."

6. Jeannine Gramick, "Rompendo o silêncio," *Época* 395 (December 12, 2005). Available at: https://oglobo.globo.com/epoca/.

7. CCE, "Instruction Concerning the Criteria for the Discernment of Vocations," nn. 1, 3.

8. ITC (International Theological Commission), "*Sensus Fidei* in the Life of the Church," Rome, 2014, n. 78. Available at: www.vatican.va.

9. Karl Lehmann, "Le service presbytéral requiert l'homme tout entire," *La documentation catholique* 2349 (2006): 36.

10. Timothy Radcliffe, "Can Gays Be Priests?" *The Tablet*, November 26, 2005. Available at: http://www.ldysinger.com/@magist/1978_SCCEd/02_radclif-com.htm.

11. CDES, "Déclaration de la Conférence des évêques suisses: La chasteté indépendamment de l'orientation sexuelle," *La documentation catholique* 2349 (2006): 33.

12. CCE, "Guidelines for the Use of Psychology in the Admission and Formation of Candidates for the Priesthood," Rome, 2007, n. 10. Available at: www.vatican.va.

13. Donald B. Cozzens, *The Changing Face of the Priesthood: A Reflection on the Priest's Crisis of Soul* (Collegeville, MN: Liturgical Press, 2000), 20, 80.

14. José Lisboa Moreira de Oliveira, *Acompanhamento de vocações homossexuais* (São Paulo: Paulus, 2007), 5.

15. Oliveira, *Acompanhamento*, 89.

16. John Boswell, "Homosexuality and Religious Life: A Historical Approach," in *Homosexuality in the Priesthood and the Religious Life*, ed. Jeannine Gramick (New York: Crossroad, 1989), 9.

17. Cozzens, *Changing Face of the Priesthood*, 79.

18. Oliveira, *Acompanhamento*, 23–25.

19. Eduardo L. Azpitarte, *Amor, sexualidade y matrimonio: Para una fundamentación de la ética cristiana* (Buenos Aires: San Benito, 2004), 80.

20. Eduardo L. Azpitarte, *Ética sexual: Masturbação, homossexualismo, relações pré-matrimoniais* (São Paulo: Paulinus, 1991), 65–66.

21. Pope Francis, "Morning Meditation in the Chapel of the Domus Sanctae Marthae: Never Slaves of the Law," October 24, 2016. Available at: www.vatican.va.

22. Pope Francis, "Morning Meditation in the Chapel of the Domus Sanctae Marthae: Rigid but Honest," May 5, 2017. Available at: www.vatican.va.

23. Cozzens, *Changing Face of the Priesthood*, 101, 109.

24. See *Catechism of the Catholic Church*, 1997, n. 2337.

25. Donald Georgen, "Calling Forth a Healthy Chaste Life," *Review for Religious* 57, no. 3 (1998): 268, in Cozzens, *Changing Face of the Priesthood*, 109–10.

26. Oliveira, *Acompanhamento*, 90–91, 6–7.

27. Cozzens, *Changing Face of the Priesthood*, 109–10.

28. Pope Francis, "The Holy Father Francis' Concluding Address at the Meeting on 'The Protection of Minors in the Church,'" Vatican, February 24, 2019. Available at: press.vatican.va.

29. Fred Daley, "I Came Out as a Gay, Catholic Priest on the Feast of the Annunciation," *America Magazine*, March 23, 2018. Available at: www.americamagazine.org.

30. Gregory Greiten, "Parish Priest Breaks the Silence, Shares That He Is Gay," *National Catholic Reporter*, December 18, 2017. Available at: www.ncronline.org.

31. Greiten, "Parish Priest Breaks the Silence."

32. Pope Francis, "Address of His Holiness Pope Francis to the General Assembly of the Italian Bishops Conference," Rome, May 21, 2018. Available at: www.vatican.va.

CHAPTER 5

1. "Respuestas de la conferencia [episcopal] alemana (al nuevo cuestionario)," *Amoris Laetitia*, April 20, 2015. Available at: sinodofamilia2015.wordpress.com.

2. CDES, "Rapport de l'Église Catholique de Suisse sur les questions concernant les lineamenta au Synode des Évêques 2015 à Rome," May 5, 2015, n. 40. Available at: www.eveques.ch.

3. Juan Masiá, "Sexualidad pluriforme y pastoral inclusiva," *Religión Digital*, March 4, 2015. Available at: https://www.religiondigital.org/convivencia_de_religiones/Sexualidad-pluriforme-pastoral-inclusiva_7_1662203780.html.

4. Juan Masiá, "Sexualidad pluriforme y educación inclusiva en la vida de las comunidades cristianas," June 21, 2015. Available at: https://crismhom.org/sexualidad-pluriforme-y-educacion-inclusiva-en-la-vida-de-las-comunidades-cristianas/.

5. Todd Salzman and Michael Lawler, "Sinalização do início de abertura na Igreja," *IHU Online* 483 (2016): 27–31. Available at: www.ihuonline.unisinos.br.

6. See Wikipedia's "Legal Status of Same-Sex Marriage" entry, https://en.wikipedia.org/wiki/Legal_status_of_same-sex_marriage. See also "Churches Divided over Amsterdam's Same-Sex Weddings," *Christianity Today*, April 1, 2001.

7. Juan Masiá, "Will Churches Bless Civilly Married LGBT?" *Vivir y pensar en la frontera* (blog), October 23, 2015. Available at: https://www.religiondigital.org/convivencia_de_religiones/Bendeciran-iglesias-parejas-LGTB-civilmente_7_1730596947.html.

8. CELAM (Latin American Episcopal Conference), *The Aparecida Document: V General Conference of the Episcopate of Latin America and the Caribbean* (Final Document), Aparecida, São Paulo. May 13–31, 2007, n. 402. Available at: https://www.celam.org/aparecida/Ingles.pdf.

9. CNPF (Comissão Nacional de Pastoral Familiar), *Manual de bioética: "chaves para a bioética"* (Brasília, DF, 2013), 68, 71.

10. CNBB, *"Homem e mulher os criou": A identidade de gênero na antropologia cristã. Orientações pastorais* (Brasília: CNBB, 2019), 17–18.

11. CNBB, *"Homem e mulher os criou,"* 27, 32.

12. Inês Castilho, "Judith Butler: Queer para um mundo não binário," September 18, 2015. Available at: https://www-ihu-unisinos-br.translate.goog/categorias/169-noticias-2015/546893-judith-butler-queer-para-um-mundo-nao-binario?_x_tr_sl=pt&_x_tr_tl=en&_x_tr_hl=en&_x_tr_pto=sc.

13. Judith Butler, "Sem medo de fazer gênero: Entrevista com a filósofa americana Judith Butler" (entrevista a Úrsula Passos). September 20, 2015. See https://teologicalatinoamericana.com/?p=1938.

14. Judith Butler, "Judith Butler escreve sobre sua teoria de gênero e o ataque sofrido no Brasil," November 19, 2017. Available at: www1.folha.uol.com.br.

15. Judith Butler, "La invención de la palabra" (interview by Milagros Belgrano Rawson), *Pagina 12*, May 8, 2009. Available at: https://www.pagina12.com.ar/diario/suplementos/soy/1-742-2009-05-08.html.

16. Pope John Paul II, *Redemptoris Missio*, encyclical letter, Rome, 1990, n. 28. Available at: www.vatican.va.

17. Aquinas, *Commentary on Aristotle's Nicomachean Ethics*, V.12. n.1019.

18. See Giannino Piana, *Introduzione all'etica cristiana* (Brescia: Queriniana, 2014).

19. "Resolução n. 11, de 18 dez. 2014," *Diário Oficial da União*, March 12, 2015, no. 48, section 1, p. 2. Available at: www.lex.com.br.

20. MEC (Ministério da Educação). "Resolução CNE/CP 1/2018," *Diário Oficial da União*, Brasília, January 22, 2018, section 1, p. 17. Available at: www.direito.mppr.mp.br.

21. ITC, "In Search of a Universal Ethic: A New Look at the Natural Law," n. 10, Rome, 2009. Available at: https://www.vatican.va/roman_curia/congregations/cfaith/cti_documents/rc_con_cfaith_doc_20090520_legge-naturale_en.html.

22. Benedict XVI, "Interview of the Holy Father Benedict XVI in Preparation for the Upcoming Journey to Bavaria," August 5, 2006. Available at: https://www.vatican.va/content/benedict-xvi/en/speeches/2006/august/documents/hf_ben-xvi_spe_20060805_intervista.html.

23. See Delumeau, *Sin and Fear*.

24. Karl Rahner, "El cristiano mayor de edad," *Razón y fe* 1 (1982): 33–43.

25. Heinrich Denzinger, *Enchiridion Symbolorum: Compendium of Creeds, Definitions, and Declarations on Matters of Faith and Morals*, ed. Peter Hünermann (San Francisco: Ignatius Press, 2012), nos. 3512–14.

26. Pope Pius X, *Fin Dalla Prima*, motu proprio, n. III, Rome, December 18, 1903. Available at: www.vatican.va.

27. ITC, "*Sensus fidei* in the Life of the Church," nos. 1–2, 50, 54.

28. ITC, "*Sensus fidei* in the Life of the Church," nos. 64–65, 70–71.

29. See ITC, "*Sensus fidei* in the Life of the Church," n. 73.

30. See ITC, "*Sensus fidei* in the Life of the Church," nos. 80, 123.

31. Rembert Truluck, *Steps to Recovery from Bible Abuse* (Gaithersburg: Chi Rho Press, 2000), vii–ix. See also A. Musskopf, "*Queer*: teoria, hermenêutica e corporeidade," in: *Teologia e sexualidade: Um ensaio contra a exclusão moral*, ed. José Trasferetti (Campina, SP: Átomo, 2004), 190–91.

32. USCCB, "Ministry to Persons with a Homosexual Inclination: Guidelines for Pastoral Care" (Washington, DC: USCCB, 2006), 22, n.44. Available at: www.usccb.org.

33. See GNRC (Global Network of Rainbow Catholics). Available at: rainbowcatholics.org.

34. Pope Francis, "Letter of His Holiness Pope Francis to the Grand Chancellor of the 'Pontificia Universidad Católica Argentina'

for the 100th Anniversary of the Founding of the Faculty of Theology," March 3, 2015. Available at: www.vatican.va.

CHAPTER 6

1. Pope Francis, "Address of His Holiness Pope Francis to Participants at the World Congress of the International Association of Penal Law," Vatican, November 15, 2019. Available at: www.vatican.va.

2. See Leroy Aarons, *Prayers for Bobby: A Mother's Coming to Terms with the Suicide of Her Gay Son* (New York: HarperCollins, 1995).

3. From the movie, *Prayers for Bobby*, based on the book by Leroy Aarons, directed by Russell Mulcahy, written by Katie Ford, Lifetime Television, January 24, 2009. See https://www.imdb.com/title/tt1073510/characters/nm0000244.

4. Justin Parkinson, "The Rise of the Rainbow Flag?," *BBC News*, June 16, 2016. Available at: https://www.bbc.com/news/magazine-36538429.

5. Portuguese original: *FAZE DE MIM UM ARCO-ÍRIS / que acolha toda as cores / em que se fragmenta / a Tua luz! / Faze de mim, sempre mais, / um arco-íris / que anuncie a bonança / depois das tempestades....* From Hélder Câmara, *Mil razões para viver: Meditações do padre José* [A thousand reasons to live: meditations by Father José] (Rio de Janeiro: Brazilian Civilization, 1978).

BIBLIOGRAPHY

AARONS, L. *Prayers for Bobby: A Mother's Coming to Terms with the Suicide of Her Gay Son*. New York: HarperCollins, 1995.

ALVES, J. *Direito romano*. Rio de Janeiro: Forense, 1977.

AMIGOS & TRIBOS. Repost of Julio Lancellotti (n.d.), Facebook, June 10, 2015. Available at: https://www.facebook.com/photo?fbid=666055623525398&set=a.148340121963620.

AQUINAS, T. *Commentary on the Nicomachean Ethics*. 2 vols. Chicago: Henry Regnery Company, 1964. Available at: https://isidore.co/aquinas/english/Ethics.htm.

ARC INTERNATIONAL. "Introduction," *Yogyakarta Principles*. 2016. Available at: https://yogyakartaprinciples.org/introduction/.

AUGUSTINE OF HIPPO. *City of God*. Project Gutenberg, 2014. Available at: https://www.gutenberg.org.

AZEVEDO, M. DE C. *Entroncamentos e entrechoques: Vivendo a fé em um mundo plural*. São Paulo, Loyola, 1991.

AZNAR G. F., and R. FEDERICO. "Las parejas no casadas: Nota a propósito de algunas publicaciones recientes." *Revista española de derecho canónico* 53 (1996): 811–22.

AZPITARTE, E. L. *Ética sexual: Masturbação, homossexualismo, relações pré-matrimoniais*. São Paulo: Paulus, 1991.

BEAUVOIR, S. DE. *A força da idade*. Rio de Janeiro: Nova Fronteira, 2009.

———. *O segundo sexo*. São Paulo: Difusão Europeia do Livro, 1970.

BENEDICT XVI. "Address of His Holiness Benedict XVI to the Participants in the International Congress on Natural Moral Law." Rome, February 12, 2007. Available at: https://www.vatican.va/

content/benedict-xvi/en/speeches/2007/february/documents/hf_ben-xvi_spe_20070212_pul.html.
———. "Address to the Members of the Roman Curia for the Traditional Exchange of Christmas Greetings." Rome, December 22, 2008. Available at: www.vatican.va.
———. *Caritas in Veritate*. Encyclical letter. Rome, June 29, 2009. Available at: https://www.vatican.va/content/benedict-xvi/en/encyclicals/documents/hf_ben-xvi_enc_20090629_caritas-in-veritate.html.
———. "Carta do santo padre Bento XVI." In *Youcat – Brasil: Catecismo jovem da Igreja Católica*. São Paulo: Paulus, 2011.
———. "General Audience." Rome, April 26, 2006. Available at: https://www.vatican.va/content/benedict-xvi/en/audiences/2006/documents/hf_ben-xvi_aud_20060426.html.
———. "Interview in Preparation for the Upcoming Journey to Bavaria." August 5, 2006. Available at: https://www.vatican.va/content/benedict-xvi/en/speeches/2006/august/documents/hf_ben-xvi_spe_20060805_intervista.html.
———. *Verbum Domini*. Post-synodal exhortation. Rome, September 30, 2010. Available at: https://www.vatican.va/content/benedict-xvi/en/apost_exhortations/documents/hf_ben-xvi_exh_20100930_verbum-domini.html.
BENTO, B. "Queer o quê? Ativismo e estudos transviados." *Cult* 193 (2014): 42–46.
BOBBIO, N. *A era dos direitos*. Rio de Janeiro: Campus, 1992.
BOSWELL, J. *Christianity, Social Tolerance, and Homosexuality: Gay People in Western Europe from the Beginning of the Christian Era to the Fourteenth Century*. Chicago: University of Chicago Press, 2015.
———. "Homosexuality and Religious Life: A Historical Approach." In *Homosexuality in the Priesthood and the Religious Rife*. Edited by Jeannine Gramick. New York: Crossroad, 1989.
———. *Same-Sex Unions in Pre-modern Europe*. New York: Villard Books, 1994.
BUTLER, J. "Como os corpos se tornam matéria: Entrevista com Judith Butler." Interview by Baukje Prins and Irene Costera. *Estudos feministas* 10, no. 1 (2002): 155–67.
———. *Gender Trouble: Feminism and the Subversion of Identity*. New York: Routledge, 2006.

———. "Judith Butler escreve sobre sua teoria de gênero e o ataque sofrido no Brasil." November 19, 2017. Available at: www1.folha.uol.com.br.

———. "La invención de la palabra." Interview by Milagros Belgrano Rawson. *Pagina 12*, May 8, 2009. Available at: https://www.pagina12.com.ar/diario/suplementos/soy/1-742-2009-05-08.html.

———. "Sem medo de fazer gênero: Entrevista com a filósofa americana Judith Butler" (entrevista a Úrsula Passos). September 20, 2015.

CALVEZ, J.-Y. "Morale sociale et morale sexuelle." *Études* 3785 (1993): 641–50.

CÂMARA, H. *Mil razões para viver: Meditações do padre José*. Rio de Janeiro: Civilização Brasileira, 1978.

"Carta a uma fundamentalista." 2007. Available at: www.diversidadesexual.com.br.

CASTILHO, I. "Judith Butler: Queer para um mundo não binário." September 18, 2015. Available at: https://www-ihu-unisinos-br.translate.goog/categorias/169-noticias-2015/546893-judith-butler-queer-para-um-mundo-nao-binario?_x_tr_sl=pt&_x_tr_tl=en&_x_tr_hl=en&_x_tr_pto=sc.

CATECISMO ROMANO (1566). Petrópolis: Vozes, 1951.

CC (CONGREGATION FOR THE CLERGY). "The Gift of the Priestly Vocation." Vatican, 2016. Available at: www.clerus.va.

CCC (*Catechism of the Catholic Church*). Rome: 1997 (First edition, provisional: 1992). Available at: www.vatican.va.

CCE (CONGREGATION FOR CATHOLIC EDUCATION). "Instruction Concerning the Criteria for the Discernment of Vocations with Regard to Persons with Homosexual Tendencies in view of their Admission to the Seminary and to Holy Orders." Vatican, 2005. Available at: www.vatican.va.

———. "Guidelines for the Use of Psychology in the Admission and Formation of Candidates for the Priesthood." Rome, 2007. Available at: www.vatican.va.

———. "'Male and Female He Created Them': Towards a Path of Dialogue on the Question of Gender Theory in Education." Vatican, 2019. Available at: www.vatican.va.

CCL: *Code of Canon Law*. Braga: Secretariado Nacional do Apostolado da Oração, 1983. Available at: www.vatican.va.

CDES (CONFERENCE OF SWISS BISHOPS). "Note pastorale 10: position de la Conférence des Évêques Suisses concernant la bénédiction par l'Église de couples homosexuels et l'engagement par l'Église de personnes vivant en partenariat homosexuel." Fribourg, 2002. Available at: www.eveques.ch.

———. "Déclaration de la Conférence des évêques suisses: la chasteté indépendamment de l'orientation sexuelle." *La documentation catholique* 2349 (2006).

———. "Rapport de l'Église Catholique de Suisse sur les questions concernant les lineamenta au Synode des Évêques 2015 à Rome." May 5, 2015. Available at: www.eveques.ch.

CDF (CONGREGATION FOR THE DOCTRINE OF THE FAITH). "Considerations Regarding Proposals to Give Legal Recognition to Unions Between Homosexual Persons." Rome, June 3, 2003. Available at: www.vatican.va.

———. Instruction *Libertatis Conscientia* on Christian freedom and liberation. Rome, 1986. Available at: http://www.vatican.va.

———. "Letter to the Bishops of the Catholic Church on the Collaboration of Men and Women in the Church and in the World." Rome, May 31, 2004. Available at: www.vatican.va.

———. "Letter to the Bishops of the Catholic Church on the Pastoral Care of Homosexual Persons—homosexualitatis problema." Rome, 1986. Available at: www.vatican.va.

———. "Some Considerations Concerning the Response to Legislative Proposals on the Non-Discrimination of Homosexual Persons." Rome, July 24, 1992. Available at: www.vatican.va.

CEF (CONFERENCE OF FRENCH BISHOPS). "Élargir le mariage aux personnes de même sexe? Ouvrons le débat!" Paris, 2012. Available at: www.eglise.catholique.fr.

CELAM (LATIN AMERICAN EPISCOPAL CONFERENCE). *The Aparecida Document: V General Conference of the Episcopate of Latin America and the Caribbean* (Final Document). Aparecida, São Paulo, May 13–31, 2007. Available at: https://www.celam.org/aparecida/Ingles.pdf.

CES (CATHOLIC EDUCATION SERVICE). *Made in God's Image: Challenging Homophobic and Biphobic Bullying in Catholic Schools*. London: St. Mary's University, 2018. Available at: www.catholiceducation.org.uk.

CHICAGO CLERGY. "An Open Letter to the Hierarchy of the Roman Catholic Church Regarding the Pastoral Care of Gay and Lesbian Persons," December 19, 2013. Available at: https://www.bishop-accountability.org/resources/resource-files/timeline/2003-12-19-Prendergast-OpenLetter.htm.

"Churches Divided over Amsterdam's Same-Sex Weddings." *Christianity Today*, April 1, 2001.

CICL (CONGREGATION FOR INSTITUTES OF CONSECRATED LIFE AND SOCIETIES OF APOSTOLIC LIFE). "Directives on Formation in Religious Institutes." Rome, 1990. Available at: https://www.vatican.va/roman_curia/congregations/ccscrlife/documents/rc_con_ccscrlife_doc_02021990_directives-on-formation_en.html.

CNBB (NATIONAL CONFERENCE OF THE BISHOPS OF BRAZIL). *Comunidade de comunidades: Uma nova paróquia*. Brasília, Edições CNBB, 2014.

———. *"Homem e mulher os criou": A identidade de gênero na antropologia cristã. Orientações pastorais*. Brasília: CNBB, 2019.

CNPF (COMISSÃO NACIONAL DE PASTORAL FAMILIAR). *Manual de bioética: "chaves para a bioética."* Brasília, DF, 2013.

COMBY, J. *From the Beginnings to the Fifteenth Century*, vol. 1 of *How to Read Church History*. New York: Crossroad, 1985.

———. *Para ler a história da Igreja: das origens ao século XV*. Vol. I. São Paulo: Loyola, 1993.

"Comunicado del obispo de Cádiz y Ceuta." September 1, 2015. Available at: w.es.catholic.net.

CONGAR, Y. *La tradition et la vie de l'Église*. Paris: Cerf, 1984.

COZZENS, D. *The Changing Face of the Priesthood: A Reflection on the Priest's Crisis of Soul*. Collegeville, MN: Liturgical Press, 2000.

CUÉ, C. E. "El Papa me pidió perdón, está espantado con los abusos, esto es un tsunami." *El País*, May 19, 2018. Available at: www.elpais.com.

DALEY, F. "I Came Out as a Gay, Catholic Priest on the Feast of the Annunciation." *America Magazine*, March 23, 2018. Available at: www.americamagazine.org.

DeBERNARDO, F. "Supreme court marriage equality case will be led by catholic gay couple." New Ways Ministry, April 21, 2015. Available at: https://www.newwaysministry.org/2015/04/21/supreme-court-marriage-equality-case-will-be-led-by-catholic-gay-couple/.

"Declaração dos direitos do homem e do cidadão" (1793). Available at: www.dhnet.org.br/direitos/anthist/dec1793.htm.

DELUMEAU, J. *À espera da aurora: Um cristianismo para o amanhã*. São Paulo: Loyola, 2007.

———. *O pecado e o medo: A culpabilização no Ocidente*. Vol. I and II. Bauru: EDUSC, 2003.

———. *Sin and Fear: The Emergence of the Western Guilt Culture, 13th–18th Centuries*. Translated by Eric Nicholson. New York: St. Martin's Press, 1990.

DEMOSTHENES. *Against Neaera*, Dem. 59 122. See *Demosthenes*. Translated by Norman W. DeWitt, and Norman J. DeWitt. Cambridge, MA: Harvard University Press, 1949.

DENZINGER, H. *Enchiridion Symbolorum: Compendium of Creeds, Definitions, and Declarations on Matters of Faith and Morals*. Edited by Peter Hünermann. San Francisco: Ignatius Press, 2012.

"Difesa dei diritti e ideologia." *L'Osservatore Romano*. December 20, 2008. Available at: tuespetrus.wordpress.com.

DUPONT, G. "Relator de projeto favorável ao casamento gay na França se diz confiante, apesar de sofrer ameaças." *Boletim eletrônico IHU*, January 30, 2013. Available at: www.ihu.unisinos.br.

FÉRAY, J.-C. "Une histoire critique du mot homosexualité." *Revue Arcadie* (March–April 1981). Available at: http://culture-et-debats.over-blog.com/article-histoire-critique-homosexualite-par-jean-claude-feray-61410181.html.

FRANCIS. "Address of His Holiness Pope Francis to Participants in the Convention Sponsored by the Congregation for the Clergy on the 50th Anniversary of the Conciliar Decrees 'Optatam Totius' And 'Presbyterorum Ordinis,'" Rome, November 20, 2015. Available at: www.vatican.va.

———. "Address of His Holiness Pope Francis to the General Assembly of the Italian Bishops Conference." Rome, May 21, 2018. Available at: www.vatican.va.

———. "Address to Participants in the Meeting Promoted by the Pontifical Council for Promoting the New Evangelization." Rome, October 11, 2017. Available at: www.vatican.va.

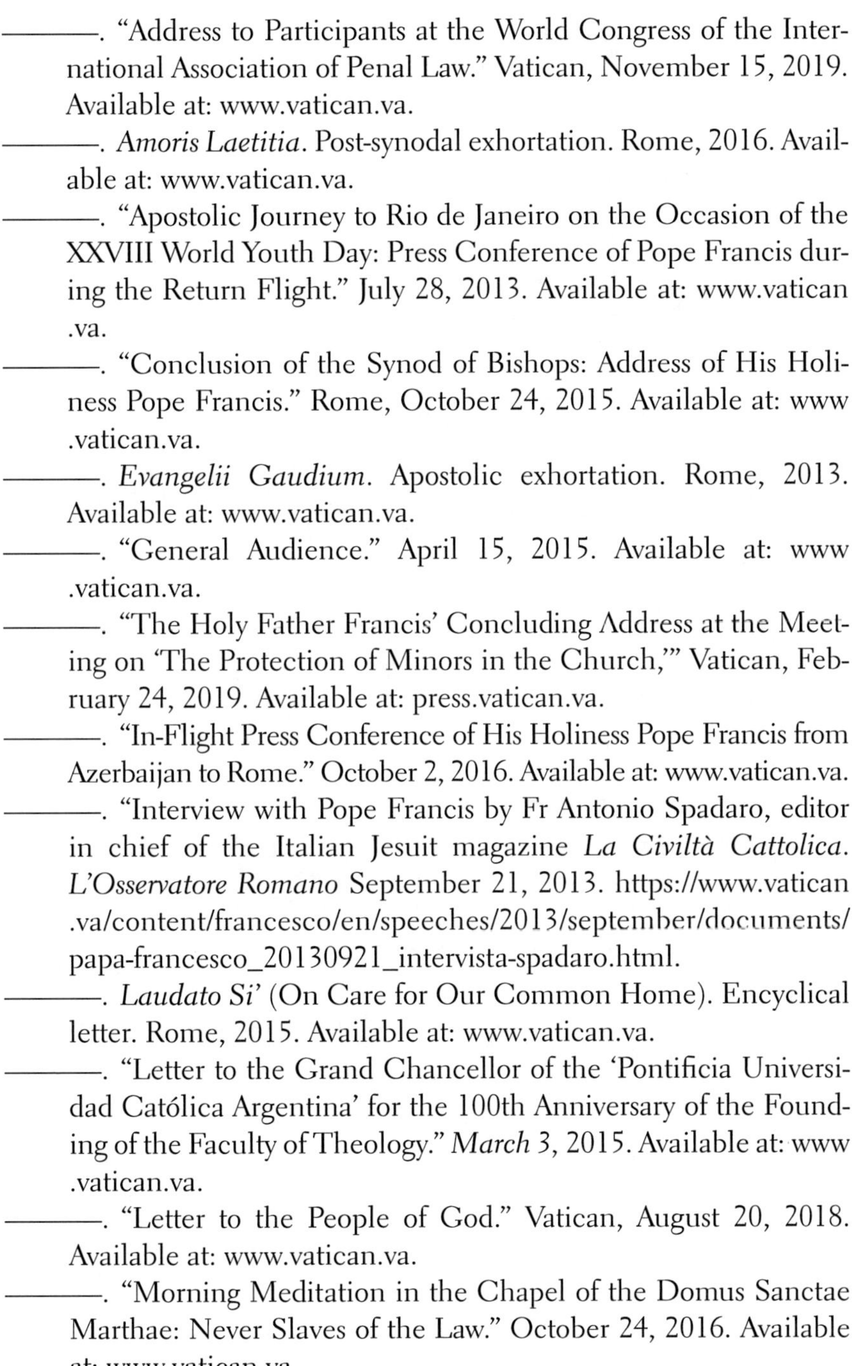

———. "Address to Participants at the World Congress of the International Association of Penal Law." Vatican, November 15, 2019. Available at: www.vatican.va.

———. *Amoris Laetitia*. Post-synodal exhortation. Rome, 2016. Available at: www.vatican.va.

———. "Apostolic Journey to Rio de Janeiro on the Occasion of the XXVIII World Youth Day: Press Conference of Pope Francis during the Return Flight." July 28, 2013. Available at: www.vatican.va.

———. "Conclusion of the Synod of Bishops: Address of His Holiness Pope Francis." Rome, October 24, 2015. Available at: www.vatican.va.

———. *Evangelii Gaudium*. Apostolic exhortation. Rome, 2013. Available at: www.vatican.va.

———. "General Audience." April 15, 2015. Available at: www.vatican.va.

———. "The Holy Father Francis' Concluding Address at the Meeting on 'The Protection of Minors in the Church,'" Vatican, February 24, 2019. Available at: press.vatican.va.

———. "In-Flight Press Conference of His Holiness Pope Francis from Azerbaijan to Rome." October 2, 2016. Available at: www.vatican.va.

———. "Interview with Pope Francis by Fr Antonio Spadaro, editor in chief of the Italian Jesuit magazine *La Civiltà Cattolica*. *L'Osservatore Romano* September 21, 2013. https://www.vatican.va/content/francesco/en/speeches/2013/september/documents/papa-francesco_20130921_intervista-spadaro.html.

———. *Laudato Si'* (On Care for Our Common Home). Encyclical letter. Rome, 2015. Available at: www.vatican.va.

———. "Letter to the Grand Chancellor of the 'Pontificia Universidad Católica Argentina' for the 100th Anniversary of the Founding of the Faculty of Theology." *March* 3, 2015. Available at: www.vatican.va.

———. "Letter to the People of God." Vatican, August 20, 2018. Available at: www.vatican.va.

———. "Morning Meditation in the Chapel of the Domus Sanctae Marthae: Never Slaves of the Law." October 24, 2016. Available at: www.vatican.va.

———. "Morning Meditation in the Chapel of the Domus Sanctae Marthae: Rigid but Honest." May 5, 2017. Available at: www.vatican.va.

———. "Solemnity of Pentecost Holy Mass with the Ecclesial Movements: Homily of Pope Francis." Rome, May 19, 2013. Available at: www.vatican.va.

———. "Video Message to Participants in an International Theological Congress Held at the Pontifical Catholic University of Argentina." Buenos Aires, September 1–3, 2015. Available at: www.vatican.va.

GEORGEN, D. "Calling Forth a Healthy Chaste Life." *Review for Religious* 57, no. 3 (1998): 260–74.

GOMES DE JESUS, J. "Orientações sobre identidade de gênero: Conceitos e termos," *Guia técnico sobre pessoas transexuais, travestis e demais transgêneros, para formadores de opinião* 2 (2012).

GNRC (GLOBAL NETWORK OF RAINBOW CATHOLICS). Available at: rainbowcatholics.org.

GRAMICK, J. "Rompendo o silêncio." *Época* 395 (December 12, 2005). Available at: https://oglobo.globo.com/epoca/.

GRANADA, VENERABLE L. OF. *The Sinner's Guide*. Translated by Fr. Charles Hyacinth McKenna. Charlotte, NC: TAN Books, 2014.

GREEN, J. N., and R. POLITO. *Frescos trópicos: Fontes sobre a homossexualidade masculina no Brasil (1870–1980)*. Rio de Janeiro: José Olympio, 2006.

GREITEN, G. "Parish Priest Breaks the Silence, Shares That He Is Gay." *National Catholic Reporter*, December 18, 2017. Available at: www.ncronline.org.

GROCHOLEWSKI, Z. "Quando não é oportuno admitir ao sacerdócio." *30 dias* 11 (2005): 24–26.

HALL, S. *A identidade cultural na pós-modernidade*. Rio de Janeiro: DP&A, 2001.

HÄRING, B. "Sessualità." In *Dizionario enciclopedico di teologia morale*. Edited by L. Rossi and A. Valsecchi. Rome: Paoline, 1973.

HERCULANO-HOUZEL, S. "O cérebro homossexual." *Folha de São Paulo* 165 (July 2006): 46–51.

HERNÁNDEZ, A. B. "El bendito encuentro entre Francisco y Diego." *Hoy*. January 25, 2015. Available at: www.hoy.es.

IRIGARAY, H. A. R. "Gays no mundo corporativo: Rompendo o pacto do silêncio." *O social em questão* 20 (2008): 110–41.

ITC (INTERNATIONAL THEOLOGICAL COMMISSION). "In Search of a Universal Ethic: A New Look at the Natural Law." Rome, 2009. Available at: https://www.vatican.va/roman_curia/congregations/cfaith/cti_documents/rc_con_cfaith_doc_20090520_legge-naturale_en.html.

———. "*Sensus Fidei* in the Life of the Church." Rome, 2014. Available at: www.vatican.va.

JOHN XXIII. *Pacem in Terris*. Encyclical letter. Rome, April 11, 1963. Available at: https://www.vatican.va/content/john-xxiii/en/encyclicals/documents/hf_j-xxiii_enc_11041963_pacem.html.

———. "Solemn Opening of the Second Vatican Council: Address of His Holiness Pope John XXIII." Vatican, October 11, 1962. Available at: https://www.vatican.va/content/john-xxiii/it/speeches/1962/documents/hf_j-xxiii_spe_19621011_opening-council.html.

JOHN PAUL II. *Redemptoris Missio*. Encyclical letter. Rome, 1990. Available at: www.vatican.va.

JUSTIN MARTYR. *First and Second Apologies*. Ancient Christian Writers, Mahwah, NJ: Paulist Press, 1997.

KEMPIS, T. À. *Imitation of Christ*. Milwaukee: The Bruce Publishing Company, 1940. Available at: https://www.ccel.org/ccel/kempis/imitation.all.html.

LACTANTIUS. *The Divine Institutes, Books I–VII*. Washington, DC: CUA Press, 2008.

LANDES, R. *The City of Women*. Albuquerque, NM: University of New Mexico Press, [1947] 2006.

LEERS, B., and J. TRASFERETTI. *Homossexuais e ética cristã*. Campinas, SP, Brazil: Átomo, 2002.

LEHMANN, K. "Le service presbytéral requiert l'homme tout entier." *La documentation catholique* 2349 (2006).

LIMA, L. "Divorciados recasados diante dos sacramentos." *Revista Eclesiástica Brasileira* 239 (2000): 641–49.

MANCINA, C. "Simone de Beauvoir mãe do feminismo." *L'Osservatore Romano*, September 1, 2016. Available at: https://www.osservatoreromano.va/pt.html.

"Mariage pour tous, un progrès humain." *Témoignage Chrétien*, December 14, 2012. Available at: https://temoignagechretien.fr.

MARTINI, C. M., and G. SPORCHILL. *Diálogos noturnos em Jerusalém: Sobre o risco da fé*. São Paulo: Paulus; Rio de Janeiro: PUC-Rio, 2008.

MARTYR, ST. JUSTIN. *First and Second Apologies*. Ancient Christian Writers. Mahwah, NJ: Paulist Press, 1997.

MASIÁ, J. "¿Bendecirán las iglesias a parejas LGTB casadas civilmente?" October 23, 2015. Available at: https://www.religiondigital.org/convivencia_de_religiones/Bendeciran-iglesias-parejas-LGTB-civilmente_7_1730596947.html.

———. "Sexualidad pluriforme y educación inclusiva en la vida de las comunidades cristianas," June 21, 2015. Available at: https://crismhom.org/sexualidad-pluriforme-y-educacion-inclusiva-en-la-vida-de-las-comunidades-cristianas/.

———. "Sexualidad pluriforme y pastoral inclusiva." *Religión Digital*. March 4, 2015. Available at: www.religiondigital.org.

MEC (MINISTÉRIO DA EDUCAÇÃO). "Resolução CNE/CP 1/2018." *Diário Oficial da União*. Brasília, January 22, 2018. Available at: www.direito.mppr.mp.br.

MONTEIRO DA VIDE, S. *Constituições primeiras do arcebispado da Bahia* (First Constitutions of the Archbishopric of Bahia). Brasília: Federal Senate, Editorial Board, 2007.

MOSER, A. "Apenas questão de gênero"? *Revista Eclesiástica Brasileira* 76, no. 301 (2016): 44–74.

MUSSKOPF, A. "*Queer*: teoria, hermenêutica e corporeidade." In *Teologia e sexualidade: Um ensaio contra a exclusão moral*, edited by José Trasferetti, 179–210. Campina, SP: Átomo, 2004.

NEOTTI, C. *Cem anos da revista de cultura Vozes*. São Paulo, 2007. Available at: www.intercom.org.br.

OAB (ORDEM DOS ADVOGADOS DO BRASIL—CONSELHO FEDERAL [Brazilian Bar Association – Federal Council]). "Anteprojeto estatuto da diversidade sexual e de gênero" [Draft sexual and gender diversity statute], 2017.

OBAMA, B. "Inaugural Address by President Barack Obama." Washington, DC, January 21, 2013. Available at: www.obamawhitehouse.archives.gov.

OCQ (OFFICE DE CATÉCHÈSE DU QUÉBEC). *La force des rencontres. Homme et femme il les créa*. Montréal: Fides, 1976. In DURAND, G. *Sexualidade e fé: Síntese de teologia moral*. São Paulo: Loyola, 1989.

OLIVEIRA, J. L. M. DE. *Acompanhamento de vocações homossexuais*. São Paulo: Paulus, 2007.
ORAISON, M. *Reconciliación: memorias*. Salamanca: Sigueme, 1969.
"Ordenações filipinas on-line" (text of 1603). Available at: http://www1.ci.uc.pt/ihti/proj/filipinas.
PARKINSON, J. "The Rise of the Rainbow Flag?" *BBC News*, June 16, 2016. Available at: https://www.bbc.com/news/magazine-36538429.
PAUL VI. *Humanae Vitae*. Encyclical letter. Rome, July 25, 1968. Available at: https://www.vatican.va/content/paul-vi/en/encyclicals/documents/hf_p-vi_enc_25071968_humanae-vitae.html.
PBC (PONTIFICAL BIBLICAL COMMISSION). "'What is Man?' (Psalm 8:5): An Itinerary through Biblical Anthropology," Vatican, 2019. Available at: www.vatican.va.
PCF (PONTIFÍCIO CONSELHO PARA A FAMÍLIA). "Familia y Derechos Humanos." Vatican, 1999. Available at: www.vatican.va.
PIANA, G. *Introduzione all'etica cristiana*. Brescia: Queriniana, 2014.
PIUS X. *Fin Dalla Prima*. Motu proprio. Rome, December 18, 1903. Available at: www.vatican.va.
PIUS XI. *Casti Connubii*. Encyclical letter on Christian marriage. Rome, 1930. Available at: https://www.vatican.va/content/pius-xi/en/encyclicals/documents/hf_p-xi_enc_19301231_casti-connubii.html.
PIUS XII. *Divino Afflante Spiritu*. Encyclical letter on promoting biblical studies. Rome, September 30, 1943. Available at: https://www.vatican.va/content/pius-xii/en/encyclicals/documents/hf_p-xii_enc_30091943_divino-afflante-spiritu.html.
———. *Moral Questions Affecting Married Life: The Apostolate of the Midwife*. New York: Paulist Press, 1951.
POMPEU, R. "Questionário para heterossexuais." *Caros amigos*. May 2008. Available at: https://sapatariadf.wordpress.com/category/mundo-diverso/page/2/.
RADCLIFFE, T. "Can Gays Be Priests?" *The Tablet*. November 26, 2005. Available at: http://www.ldysinger.com/@magist/1978_SCCEd/02_radclif-com.htm.
RAHNER, K. "El cristiano mayor de edad." *Razón y fe* 1 (1982): 33–43.
RATZINGER, J. "Hacia una teología del matrimonio." *Selecciones de teologia* 35 (1970): 237–48.

———. "The Transmission of Divine Revelation." In *Commentary on the Documents of Vatican II*. Edited by H. Vorgrimler. Vol. 3. New York: Herder, 1969.

"Resolução n. 11, de 18 dez. 2014." *Diário Oficial da União*. March 12, 2015, n. 48, section 1, p. 2. Available at: www.lex.com.br.

"Respuestas de la conferencia [episcopal] alemana (al nuevo cuestionario)," *Amoris Laetitia*, April 20, 2015. Available at: sinodofamilia2015.wordpress.com.

ROUGHGARDEN, J. "Homossexualidade como traço adaptativo." *Mente & cérebro* 185, (2008): 50–55.

SALZMAN, T., and M. LAWLER. *The Sexual Person: Toward a Renewed Catholic Anthropology*. Moral Traditions. Washington, DC: Georgetown University Press, 2008.

———. "Sinalização do início de abertura na Igreja." *IHU On-line* 483 (2016). Available at: www.ihuonline.unisinos.br.

SECOND VATICAN COUNCIL. *Dei Verbum* (Dogmatic Constitution on Divine Revelation). Rome, 1965. Available at: www.vatican.va.

———. *Gaudium et Spes* (Pastoral Constitution on the Church in the Modern World). Rome, 1965. Available at: www.vatican.va.

———. *Unitatis Redintegratio* (Decree on Ecumenism). Rome, 1964. Available at: www.vatican.va.

SEGNI, L. DEI (Pope Innocent III). *De miseria condicionis humane*. Edited by Robert E. Lewis. Athens: The University of Georgia Press, 1978.

SNOEK, J. "Eles também são da nossa estirpe: Considerações sobre a homofilia." *Revista Vozes* (September 1967): 792–803. Available at: www.diversidadesexual.com.br.

SOARES DE SOUSA, G. *Tratado descritivo do Brasil em 1587* (Descriptive Treatise of Brazil in 1857). Rio de Janeiro: Laemmert's Universal Typographia, 1851.

"Statement of the Holy See Delegation at the 63rd Session of the General Assembly of the United Nations on the Declaration on Human Rights, Sexual Orientation and Gender Identity." December 18, 2008. Available at: www.vatican.va.

SYNOD OF BISHOPS. "Pastoral Challenges to the Family in the Context of Evangelization. Preparatory Document. Vatican, 2013. Available at: www.vatican.va.

TRULUCK, R. *Steps to Recovery from Bible Abuse*. Gaithersburg: Chi Rho Press, 2000.

United Nations. "Universal Declaration of Human Rights" (1948). Available at: https://www.un.org/en/about-us/universal-declaration-of-human-rights.

USCCB (UNITED STATES CONFERENCE OF CATHOLIC BISHOPS). "Always our Children: a Pastoral Message to Parents of Homosexual Children and Suggestions for Pastoral Ministers." Washington, DC, 1997. Available at: www.usccb.org.

———. "Ministry to Persons with a Homosexual Inclination: Guidelines for Pastoral Care." Washington, DC: USCCB, 2006. Available at: www.usccb.org.

VEYNE, P. "A homossexualidade em Roma." In *Sexualidades ocidentais*, edited by Philippe Ariès and André Béjin, 39–49. São Paulo: Brasiliense, 1985.

VIDAL, M. *Sexualidade e condição homossexual na moral cristã*. Aparecida, SP, Brazil: Santuário, 2008.

VIDE, S. M. *Constituições primeiras do arcebispado da Bahia* (1707). Brasília: Senado Federal, 2007.

VIEIRA, H. "Teoría queer, ¿o que é isso?" *Fórum*, June 7, 2015. Available at: https://revistaforum.com.br.

"The Virginia Declaration of Rights" (1776). Available at: https://www.archives.gov/founding-docs/virginia-declaration-of-rights.

YOSHINO, K. *Covering: The Hidden Assault on Our Civil Rights*. New York: Random House, 2006.

INDEX